W9-ACL-684

Hemerocallis, The Daylily

Hemerocallis, The Daylily

R. W. Munson, Jr.

TIMBER PRESS
Portland, Oregon

© 1989 by Timber Press, Inc.
All rights reserved

ISBN 0-88192-140-8
Printed in Hong Kong

TIMBER PRESS, INC.
9999 SW Wilshire
Portland, Oregon 97225

Library of Congress Cataloging-in-Publication Data

Munson, R. W.
    Hemerocallis, the daylily / R.W. Munson, Jr.
        p.   cm.
    Includes indexes.
    ISBN 0-88192-140-8
    1. Daylilies.   I. Title.
SB413.D3M86   1989
635.9'34324--dc20   89-5025
                                             CIP

Contents

Preface

I have grown daylilies for over 40 years, during which time I have seen major changes occur, mostly in beauty, color and variety of form. For years I felt these changes warranted all sacrifices made, whatever they were, regarding health, vigor and stamina. Now I am not so certain. Let me share with you some thoughts and growing concerns that are changing or at least moderating this point of view.

In the early years, daylilies were what I would describe as plain, but consistent, dependable and hardy—hardy in the sense they were tough! Over the past 25–30 years the daylily has become greatly refined and can now certainly be described as unique, beautiful, and varied. But regrettably it is not as dependable as it once was and is indeed beginning to be fraught with infirmities, such as crown rot, the yellows, spring sickness, as well as a developing susceptibility to insects it never had in the early years.

One can honestly ask, "How does this happen? How can we let it happen?" There are no easy answers. It is a very complex problem, and regrettably most of the time we do not even recognize that there is a problem—and this in itself is a major part of the "problem"! From the very beginning we have taken our plant's legacy of health for granted: a God-given legacy that would not change. However, mucking around with it for 50 years or so shows that man in all his infinite wisdom can do both wondrous and not so wondrous things.

I pinpoint the beginnings of the problem with the advent of daylily shows. Not that the shows had an effect—just that they changed our focus. Previously the daylily was viewed primarily in the garden. Attention was on "garden" effect. The shows moved the daylily to the show bench, sort of from the back of the bus to the front. Here we saw the bloom up close—under a microscope, if you will. Beauty became the first and most desirable quality. With this emphasis it soon became beauty at all cost! A plant's ability to grow, increase and sustain itself became of secondary and almost minimal interest. As breeding evolved and reached a fever pitch, we had breeders using seedlings of which they knew little or nothing—i.e, how the plants would grow and perform, before they were establishing new lines.

Let me share a story with you. I met W. B. MacMillan in 1960 and we became fast friends. He was a masterful genius. Casting aside all his early work he reestablished a new program in 1960. He then set about to create the most beautiful daylilies of the day. He did so by taking three or four cultivars from diverse lines. (Munson, Fay, Kraus, Edna Spalding) and worked them in many and varied combinations. He bloomed seedlings in nine months and consequently was able to bloom three generations in three years, where most could only bloom 1 or 1½ generations at best in the same period. He certainly speeded up the changes that could be made. While visiting Mac in 1965 I saw a glorious pink seedling. I was involved with tetraploids at that time and wanted this plant to breed with my 'Incomparable' to produce seed for treating. Mac sent me the plant, to use; he was generous that way. The next year it scaped, but before blooming a "sooty" black line started up the scape. In two weeks the plant was dead, despite all the fungicides I could use. I dug down and found the roots intact, so I convinced myself it would rejuvenate and send up a new shoot. Of course, it never did. I finally admitted my loss to Mac and he in turn admitted it was a trait to which the plant was apparently subject. I was thankful no seed were set. But as Mac said he'd used it the previous two years—had seed but had not kept records, so did not know where they were. Here was a plant with a potentially lethal problem. But at least it was an obvious one—and a wise man walked away from it—admittedly perhaps two season to late.

But over the years there have been other, less obvious infirmities at work. Resolving the problem will take the patience of Job and the wisdom of Solomon. It has been a long time emerging—it will be difficult to reverse. I doubt that it can be stopped at this late date—but perhaps controlled or managed. Too many people have used too many suspect cultivars—so there are few if any "clean lines" left. Identifying the culprits is nearly impossible. But as with any illness or disease the patient must accept the fact there is a problem and until that is done there cannot be a cure. We must accept the fact that our plant may be on the verge of being quite sick. The level and complexity of the illness is not yet known—but when rot occurs in the South in established clumps without transplanting there is a problem. When a breeder lines out a year's selected seedling crop and 90% rot because lining out was done in August and not October or November, we have a problem. When we look to remedies such as sprays, drenches, soaks, fungicides, etc., we have a problem!

It was my hope that tetraploids would be a sort of savior or a panacea since we had taken 10 steps backward, working with rather primitive cultivars or induced plants, to go forward again. But this fantasy was short-lived as I see the increased desire (almost at a frenzy now) to convert the very latest and most exotic diploid regardless of any latent tendencies toward infirmities or lack of stamina. We are again at the crossroads where beauty is sought at all cost and at the greatest possible speed. We are now creating tetraploids with all the latent problems our diploids possess—but none are wearing a red badge saying "I MAY BE CONTAMINATED! USE ME WITH CAUTION!" We have seen breeders in other genera march heedlessly into the future—a future dimmed because they were indifferent and their plant become too difficult to grow or too much of a "nuisance". It will be a tragedy if this happens to daylilies.

Our flower started tough, pure and clean! Is it now time to reverse the trend we have seen developing over the years, that of beauty at all costs and health will take care of itself. We must get back to basics. Let's put the daylily back into the garden! I am not a radical: I do not intend we throw the baby out with the bath water. But to ignore the growing array of signs is suicidal. And, during this period of reassessment let's admit that there is room for more than the short and the round! Tall is not bad—but tall that does not stand up is bad. Sickly is sickly and bad under any circumstances. Everything does not have to be round and ruffled; spiders and doubles are allowing us to once again broaden our daylily horizons. We are less myopic then we were 10 years ago. But it's time we cleared our vision to 20/20 and allow our plant to be all it can be. We shouldn't allow our prejudice, that which we've taught each other over the past 25 years, to dictate the daylilies which future generations will grow. Remember, each generation tends to see things differently. I believe tetraploids will unlock more avenues of variety then we will ever be able to explore or cope with, if we want them to. This in itself is very exciting and reassuring. But they will not protect us from our own ignorance or myopia as to our plant's health, vigor and vitality. It is time to pause and reflect—and then to move forward with greater resolve than ever before that our plant is unique—one of a kind and that we must protect its heritage—not squander it as if there was no tomorrow—for "if we do, there surely won't be one." If we lose our heritage of health and vigor all the beauty that has been achieved will be for naught!

Illustration Contributors

Thank you to the following contributors for the use of their illustrations:

John Mason Allgood
Darrel A. Apps
Jim April
John Benz
E. C. (Edwin C.) Brown
Clarence J. Crochet
Albert Durio
Dalton Durio
Ken (Kenneth G.) Durio
Robert D. Elliott, Jr.
Alex Goldberg
Davis Guidry
Lucille S. Guidry
Ra Hansen
Mrs. Ralph (Pauline) Henry
Howard J. Hite
Betty Hudson
Ron L. Jinkerson
Ahston Johnson
Merle O. Kent
David Kirchhoff
Harold H. Kirk
John R. Lambert

Roger L. Mercer
Bryant Millikan
Steve C. Moldovan
Morton L. Morss
Virginia L. Peck
Trudy Petree
Charles Pierce (deceased)
Sanford Roberts
Elizabeth Hudson Salter
Love Seawright
Van M. Sellers
Carl W. Sigel
Sarah Sikes
Mrs. W. H. (Ethel) Smith
Patrick Stamile
D. Steve Varner
R. L. Webster
Judith Weston
Oscie B. Whatley
Lucille Williamson (deceased)
Roy G. Woodhall
Clarke M. Yancey

Introduction

Even though the daylily has been found in other areas of the Orient, I will always think of the daylily as innately Chinese and perhaps rightly so, for the daylily has been a major garden plant in China since the first days of ancient Chinese culture. There is something uniquely beautiful about the daylily: mystical, tranquil and yet uniquely Spartan. Whether it was growing in the ancient feudal state of Wei during the Chou Dynasty (1122–255 B.C.) or in the State of Wu where it was frequently used as a gift to the grieving and melancholy; or whether growing in a formal garden in Nanking; a medieval castle in Italy or Spain; or a 20th-century garden somewhere in the United States; this pristine plant of unique qualities and a remarkable growing ability brings rewards and much joy to its grower, rewards that are both soothing to the mind and up-lifting of the spirit.

The daylily has been part of the Chinese culture for thousands of years and was used before the development of the written Chinese language. The earliest records report the plant's use for food. The first known reference to daylily is about 2697 B.C. when Emperor Huang Ti arranged for a Materia Medica to be written for him by Chi Pai, which was repeatedly rewritten until 656 A.D. Hsuan Ts'ao or daylily (or Lu Tsung as it was also called) was thought to quiet the five viscera, benefit the mind and strengthen willpower. The plants which grew wild in the woods were moved into the garden for use at the table, not unlike the way we grow and use herbs today.

The first written Chinese record about daylilies appears in one of the canonical writings of Confucianism, *The Classic of Songs* (Shih-ching). It is said Confucius (551–479 B.C.) was responsible for selecting the inclusions and for editing the manuscript.

The history of the daylily in Europe is difficult to trace because of problems in inter-preting the written record and also because of inaccuracies of various authors. There are accounts that indicate the daylily was grown in the Mediterranean and written about at the time of St. Paul. These accounts are of course inaccurate. As intriguing as the idea may be, the plant we know as *Hemerocallis* (daylily) today was not introduced into the Mediterranean area much before 1550 A.D.

References to daylilies in Europe first appeared in the works of three herbalists: Rembert Dodoens (Dodonacus 1517–1585) and Charles de l'Ecluse (l'Escluse Clausius 1526–1609), both from Belgium, and Mathias de l'Obel (de Lobel or Lobelius 1538–1616) from France. The three were extremely close friends and freely imparted their observations to one another.

The daylily appeared in these European herbals of the 16th century as Lilasphodelus, Liriosphodelus and Lilium non-bulbosum. From Lobel's accounts we know that by 1576 two daylilies had already been introduced into Europe, *H. lilioasphodelus (H. flava)* and *H. fulva.*

The actual routes used to introduce daylilies into Europe are not known, but some very plausible possibilities include the overland trade routes to Hungary taken by medieval Asian traders and settlers; routes taken by Chinese, Arabian and Phoenician traders to Venice; and the sea routes of the Portugese traders to Lisbon. The European terminus of *H. flava* appears to have been Hungary, while those of *H. fulva*'s either Lisbon or Venice.

By 1890 all the then known species of *Hemerocallis* except *H. minor* and *H. graminea* had been introduced 'to American gardens.

During the period of greatest activity in China the best known collectors were Ernest Wilson, George Forrest, Frank Kingdon Ward and Joseph Rock. These gifted, professional plant collectors each discovered that the River Gorge country in western China was a plantsman's paradise.

In 1921 a seemingly unrelated event was to greatly affect the world of daylilies. At this time Dr. Albert Steward was assigned to teach botany at the University of Nanking. Here he met and taught many of China's young botanists. His home became the meeting place of Chinese people of all ages and various backgrounds. He was able to obtain what earlier botanical explorers had not even had a chance to see. This knowledge and the free exchange of plant material was to soon establish the Steward-Stout connection. It was a major connection and ideal for the development of knowledge of *Hemerocallis*.

Dr. Stout was to receive 27 living plants and seeds from central China in 1924. In a later publication Dr. Stout recorded that between 1920–1942 he had received more than 50 importations of living plants and seeds of *Hemerocallis* from China.

A. B. Stout's contributions to the botany and horticulture of *Hemerocallis* are numerous, but perhaps the most outstanding are, 1) establishing a scientific understanding of the biology of *Hemerocallis*, and 2) opening the door to the future potential of the genus. Dr. Stout skillfully, systematically and patiently worked on hybridization of the species, and fully recorded their pedigrees. He triumphantly demonstrated that man can extract from the gene pool of *Hemerocallis* genetic factors which change the quality and the intensity of the red pigmentation and the patterns of distribution, as well as producing new combinations hitherto unknown in gardens and in nature. In doing so he increased dramatically the momentum of the movement of hybridization of *Hemerocallis*, which is being continued and greatly amplified by many breeders today.

1

Species of Daylilies

The following material depends very heavily upon Dr. A. B. Stout's book *Daylilies: The Wild Species and Garden Clones Both Old and New of the Genus* (1934). After 54 years Dr. Stout's work continues to be the definitive work on species. Though questions continue to arise, and there are those who question the classifications and prefer to list the species alphabetically, I still feel that until a more comprehensive study can be mounted, his work remains the measuring stick by which we must describe the various species. As interest in daylilies expands, an increased interest in the species will also occur. And if political and economical relations with China become more harmonious perhaps expeditions to the regions of our plant's beginnings will prove beneficial. In the meantime Dr. Stout's compendium of species amended by Dr. Shiu-Ying Hu's work must suffice.

List of Species

* Species identified by Dr. A. B. Stout
** Species identified by Dr. Shui-Ying Hu

Hemerocallis altissima Stout **
Hemerocallis aurantiaca Baker *
Hemerocallis citrina Baroni *
Hemerocallis coreana Nakai **
Hemerocallis dumortierii Morren *
Hemerocallis esculenta Koidzumi **
Hemerocallis exaltata Stout *
Hemerocallis flava Linn *
Hemerocallis Forrestii Diels *
Hemerocallis fulva Linn *
Hemerocallis graminea Andrews **
Hemerocallis hakunensis Nakai **
Hemerocallis littorea Makino **
Hemerocallis longituba Miquel *
Hemerocallis micrantha Nakai **
Hemerocallis middendorffii Trautvetter and Meyer *

Hemerocallis minor Miller *
Hemerocallis multiflora Stout *
Hemerocallis nana *
Hemerocallis pedicellata Nakai **
Hemerocallis plicata Stapf *
Hemerocallis thunbergii Baker *

Species photos in this chapter courtesy of Carl W. Sigel, 11116 Bremerton Court, Raleigh, N. C. 27613.

Of the known daylilies at least 13 distinct species are now recognized. In nearly all cases these were named and described from a few plants brought into cultivation in Europe or North America. In certain cases these plants were from the wild; in other cases they were evidently plants selected or developed from wild stock and already in cultivation in the Orient.

In the list of species, those marked with an asterisk are from Dr. Stout's book.

The listing is not verifiable and may certainly be questionable in that all are not still available and identifiable or should have been awarded the status "species". No truly significant work on species has been done since Dr. Stout's book was published 1934.

However, in 1968 Dr. Shiu-Ying Hu prepared a rather remarkable work for the *American Horticultural Magazine*, listing species additional to those of Dr. Stout. Excerpts from that work follow. Those discovered after Dr. Stout's work was published and described by Dr. Hu are marked with ** in the species list.

Description of Species

Hemerocallis nana W. W. Smith and Forrest

H. nana grows compactly with a crown of short and almost erect branches. Some of the main roots become somewhat enlarged and fleshy and, as far as the writer has observed, the fleshy part is at the end of a root and at some distance from the crown. The leaves of plants in culture may be as much as 15 in. long and are expanded rather than plicate and longer than the scapes. The scapes are slender, bending outward, and usually bear one flower. When there are two or more flowers the scape is branched. The bracts are inconspicuous and there will often be two to a scape even though there is but one flower. The flowers may have a spread of 3+ in.; the segments are rather narrow; the tube is short and not sharply defined; the color on the inner face is a clear orange, but on the reverse shades of reddish brown may appear.

This species somewhat resembles *H. dumortierii* in habit of growth and character of the flowers, but is less robust, the bracts are less conspicuous and the scapes are, when more than one-flowered, decidedly branched.

Hemerocallis plicata Stapf

This species was described as new by Stapf in 1923 and as being different from *H. nana*, in having folded leaves and more flowers to an inflorescence.

The New York Botanical Garden has obtained living plants bearing the name of this species from several sources. Few plants have bloomed well and the material has not been sufficient for adequate judgment of the specific distinctions. One plant received as *H. plicata* had a scape taller than the leaves, was loosely branched and bore eight flowers; in the face of the open flowers there was a faint but distinct halo of fulvous color; and the leaves were open not plicate.

Hemerocallis forrestii Diels

The first description of this species by Diels in 1912 reports the color of the flowers as deep reddish orange and as allied to *H. fulva* particularity to the so-called *H. fulva* var. *augustifolia* described by Baker. There has, however, been no trace of the epidermal fulvous pigment characteristic of *H. fulva* in any of the flowers of plants of this species which have bloomed at The New York Botanical Garden and which were received as living plants under this name from The Royal Botanic Gardens at Kew and from the gardens of the Royal Horticultural Society at Wisley, England.

The species *H. nana*, *H. plicata*, and *H. forrestii* appear to be dwarf or nearly dwarf daylilies discovered in southwestern China by the botanical explorer Forrest.

Hemerocallis flava Linn

Lemon Daylily, Tall Yellow Daylily, or Custard Lily. The Lemon Daylily has been a favorite garden flower in Europe for at least three and a half centuries and it remains today as one of the best of the daylilies, for there is no other yellow-flowered daylily of the same semirobust stature that blooms as early in the season.

The flowers are a uniform lemon-chrome in color, strongly and agreeably odorous, medium full, wide-spreading, of good size, and lasting well throughout the hours of daylight. Often the flowers remain fresh into a second day, in which case there are two sets open for a time—behavior called "extended blooming." The scapes are ascending and almost erect, branching at the apex, and about 3 ft. high. The foliage is abundant, medium dark green in color, and the apex of the dome of leaves is about 6 in. below the flowers.

The Lemon Daylily is the plant mentioned in botanical literature as early as 1570 under the name *Asphodelus luteus liliflorus.* It remained in cultivation and 192 years later received from Linnaeus (in 1762) its modern botanical name *Hemerocallis flava.* There are many references to this daylily in horticultural and botanical literature.

There are several different clones in cultivation under the name *H. flava* which differ somewhat from the type in stature, size of flowers, habit of growth, and shape of capsules. One of these clones has somewhat smaller flowers, scapes and foliage that are more stiffly erect, and capsules that are blunter and slightly beaked.

Hemerocallis minor Miller

Grass-leaved Daylily. There are various low-growing daylilies cultivated under the name *H. minor, H. graminea, H. gracilis,* and *H. graminifolia,* many of which are obviously either variations of *H. dumortierii* or hybrids with this species as one of the parents. But some of them are of a type that is distinct from *H. flava* and that conform closely to the first but meager description of *H. minor* by Miller in 1768.

The flowers are, on the inner face, of a uniformly lemon-chrome shade of yellow, the perianth tube is greenish, and the outside of the sepals is tinged with brownish red. The scapes are slender, ascending about 2 ft. tall, and somewhat short-branching above. The foliage is composed of slender narrow leaves 15–18 in. long, but as they are weakly ascending the mounds of foliage stand well below the flowers. The foliage dies completely to the ground early in autumn and all buds become dormant. The capsule is

H. minor. Photo by SIGEL

9

narrow elliptic in outline, somewhat triangular in cross-section, about 1½ in. in length, and its seeds are about ⅛ in. in length, the smallest size known for any species of *Hemerocallis*. Flowering occurs in early spring, beginning about 10 days later than the *H. flava*. The crown is extremely compact with short, erect branches, and rhizomes are lacking. The roots are slender, cylindrical and not fleshy, with numerous fibrous laterals which are flesh-brown in color.

This species is quite distinct from *H. flava*. It is smaller in every feature except size of flower, and its foliage dies much earlier in autumn; it is more compact in the crown; the roots are smaller, finer, and not fleshy; the capsule is more slender and the seeds much smaller.

Hemerocallis thunbergii Baker

Thunberg's Daylily, Late Yellow Daylily. A daylily was mentioned under the name *Hemerocallis thunbergii* by Peter Barr in 1873, as a plant that starts to flower somewhat later then *H. fulva* (The Europa Daylily), has flowers a clear, beautiful, yellow color, and is 3 ft. tall. This plant was first listed for sale in the catalog of Barr and Sugden in 1873.

A somewhat detailed description of this species appeared in July 1890 based on plants then being grown in the Royal Botanic Gardens at Kew, England. Baker applied the name as *Hemerocallis thunbergii* Baker Hort., which indicates that he was aware that this name was already in use for this plant in horticultural circles.

Plants of Thunberg's Daylily, of the clone widely cultivated and believed to be that named by Baker, have a robust and compact habit of growth and are strongly spreading in the crown by short, erect branches. The roots are somewhat enlarged and fleshy. The foliage is medium dark green and ascending-spreading to a general level of about 30 in., and dies in late autumn, usually not until after frost. The scapes are numerous, slender, stiffly erect to a height of about 45 in., and are well-branched above. The flowers are lemon-yellow in color with the tube and the outside of the sepals strongly tinged green; a spread of about 3 in.; and tending to fade and wilt in the afternoon during hot, sunny weather. Flowering is in midsummer; in New York it blooms in July along with the Europa Daylily and after plants of *H. flava* and *H. minor* have ceased to bloom. The capsule is broadly blunt at the apex, almost truncate, and much smaller then the capsule of *H. flava*.

Thunberg's Daylily has an excellent robust habit, attractive dark green foliage, and an abundance of flowers. It is to be classed as a good garden plant form blooming in mid-summer. It has been used rather extensively in breeding. In size of flowers and in richness and purity of yellow coloring it is perhaps surpassed or at least supplemented by various new hybrids. Thunberg's Daylily is rather widely known in American gardens.

H. thunbergii. Photo by SIGEL

H. citrina. Photo by SIGEL

Hemerocallis citrina Baroni

Citron Daylily, Long Yellow Daylily. The Citron Daylily is a distinctive type. The flowers are night-blooming or nocturnal; they begin to open shortly before sunset, are widely open during the night, and usually close early in the following forenoon, especially on warm, sunny days. They are of large size with a long tube, but the segments are narrow. The color is pale lemon-yellow; the sepals are greenish on the back and purplish at the tips, a feature especially noticeable in the bud. The flowers are fragrant and bloom in midsummer. The foliage is coarse, vigorous in growth, as long a 40 in., decidedly erect but often bending or even breaking abruptly. Its color during summer is dark green, but in autumn it dies quickly and for a time is conspicuously yellowish brown. The base of the leaves in the soil is pink or almost bright red. The scapes are stiffly erect, about 45 in. tall, and much branched near the apex, bearing numerous flowers. The writer has counted as many as 64 flower buds to a single scape. The capsules are usually about 1 in. in length, obovate, and indented and purplish at the apex. The crown is compact and without spreading rhizomes. Of the main roots many are long and slender of a diameter of about 3/16 in., but some are spindle-shaped and enlarged to a diameter of about ½ in. The younger roots are orange in color while the older main roots are almost brown.

The Citron Daylily has an excellent and robust habit of growth and an abundance of attractive, dark green foliage, but because of the night-blooming habit and the narrow segments of the flowers it is not valuable for garden use. This species has been much hybridized with various other daylilies and especially with *H. thunbergii.* Some of the seedlings, the Ophir Daylily for example, far surpass the parent in having large full flowers of good day-blooming habit and much richer color.

Hemerocallis fulva Linn

Fulvous or Tawny Daylily. Several cultivated clones and various wild types or varieties are included under the specific name *H. fulva.*

The clone 'Europa'. The oldest and the best known of the fulvous daylilies is the one commonly know as *Hemerocallis fulva* L. This single-flowered daylily was described under the name *Liriosphodelus phoeniceus* by Lobel in 1576 as having cinnabar-red coloring in the flowers and as being very distinct from the yellow-flowered daylily (*H. flava*), which was then also in cultivation in Europe. In 1601, Clusius states that this plant was being grown in many gardens throughout Austria and Germany. Nearly 200 years later, Linnaeus (1753) considered this daylily a hybrid, but a few years afterward (1762) he gave it specific rank with the name *H. fulva.*

But the plants of this particular daylily do not produce seeds from any pollination source. They have always been propagated solely by vegetative divisions so are all merely branches derived from one original seedling, thus constituting a clone. It has been suggested by the writer that the horticultural name Europa Daylily be used to designate this daylily as a horticultural clone distinct from various other of the species.

We may perhaps assume that the Daylily Europa had its origin in the Orient together with the Lemon Daylily (*H. flava*). How and when these two found their way into garden culture in Europe, where they were reported in 1567, is a matter of conjecture.

A plant of Europa Daylily is one of the most robust of daylilies. It extends itself vigorously by coarse, widely spreading rhizomes. The roots are numerous, many of them becoming enlarged and fleshy. The foliage is light green, rather coarse, strongly distichous in arrangement, and forms a dome about 3 ft. in height. In coarseness of foliage it is surpassed among the older daylilies only by the double-flowered form. The older leaves die in autumn, but younger leaves continue to appear which remain somewhat green until heavy frosts. The scapes are coarse and strong, stiffly erect to a height of about 50 in., and are branched at the top bearing as many as 15–20 flowers. The flowers have a fulvous overcast of color in the outer zone of the open flower with reticulated veins of darker shades. An arching mid-zone of darker shade in the petals is a conspicuous feature. The throat of the flower is orange only. The petals are rather thin, slightly wavy along the margin, and of delicate texture; yet they retain form and color well during the day. The segments are rather broad and overlapping, giving a full flower. The flowers are strictly day-blooming; they open after daylight and close about sunset. The season of bloom is in July. The capsule, produced only rarely and to the compatible pollen of certain cross-pollinations, is about 1 in. in length, broadly ovate, with the apex truncate and indented.

The persistent self-incompatibility of the entire clone of the Europa Daylily makes it impossible to obtain selfed seedlings. Only within very recent years has the Europa Daylily been used successfully in hybridization with other daylilies.

Double-flowered Fulvous Daylilies exist both with green foliage and with white-striped variegated foliage. They all closely resemble the Europa Daylily in the color of the flowers, in habit of growth, in diurnal habit of flowering, and in season of bloom. The first of these to be introduced into Europe was displayed under the name *"Hemerocallis disticha flore pleno"* by Veitch and Son before the Royal Horticultural Society in 1860. A few years later mention was made of a *"Hemerocallis Kwanso foliis variegatis"* which had been introduced directly from Japan by van Siebold. This was soon illustrated in a colored plate showing the white-striped foliage and a flower somewhat less double than that of the plant introduced earlier by Veitch and Son. *The Gardeners' Chronicle* in 1867 called this variegated type *"Hemerocallis Kwanso flore-pleno."* Thus it appears that the name "Kwanso" was first used for a daylily that was both variegated and double-flowered.

Plants of the variegated, double-flowered type have been secured from several sources for culture by The New York Botanical Garden. The variegation is evidently of the chimeral type, as association of green and white cells, so the plants frequently produce all-green branches and offsets which continue as purely green plants. Hence it may well be that some of the double-flowered plants with all-green foliage now in cultivation arose from the variegated Kwanso Daylily.

The New York Botanical Garden has also obtained entirely green-leaved plants under the names Kwanso and Flore-Pleno from nurserymen, other botanical gardens, and from various localities in China and Japan. These have been grown side by side for comparison and study. There seems to be no noticeable difference in the color of the flowers nor in the various aspects of growth habit. Some plants, however, have all flowers very double, while other plants have semidouble flowers. For certain of these plants various degrees of doubleness may be found on the same plant, but never has a flower produced a perfect pistil.

The propagation of the double-flowered types is solely by division, for the pistils of the flowers are transformed into a column of petals so the formation of fruit is not possible. Stamens or anthers are usually present but the pollen is mostly aborted. All of the double-flowered plants this far studied are triploids.

Of the origin of the double-flowered type there is no record. It was in existence in Japan in 1712 and is known to be rather widely distributed in Japan and to some extent also in China, both in culture and as an apparent escape, evidently quite as the Europa Daylily now exists in such old-settled areas as Long Island, about abandoned homesites, along roadsides, and wherever the activities of man have given the plant a chance to spread vegetatively. The very close relationship between the double-flowered types Kwanso, Flore-Pleno, Variegated, and the single-flowered Europa Daylily is obvious. All are triploids; they are very similar in flower-colors and habit of growth, and all are strictly diurnal in flowering habits.

When plants of the Europa Daylily are grown beside plants having double flowers the former are somewhat earlier to bloom, have foliage somewhat less coarse, and have scapes that are taller. The color of the flowers is almost the same. The zone of eye spot is, however, less developed in the smaller and inner accessory segments of the double flowers than in their more primary segments and in the petals of the single-flowered Europa Daylily.

The double-flowered daylilies have not become popular garden plants. Many gardners find the flowers monstrous, coarse, and lacking in pleasing symmetry. The Variegated Kwanso is seldom grown in American gardens. A single-flowered type with variegated foliage has been mentioned in the literature, but this has never been seen by the writer nor has it been learned where it may be obtained.

Hemerocallis disticha Donn. Evidently no fulvous daylily other than the clone 'Europa' found its way into Europe until about 1798 when the "*Hemerocallis disticha*" was obtained from China. The descriptions of this plant make it clear that it was a fulvous daylily with elongated perianth tube and narrow segments, which made it appear to be quite distinct from the Europa Daylily. It remained in cultivation, at least for some time.

Hemerocallis longituba Miquel. In 1867 the Dutch botanist Miquel described certain herbarium specimens as a new species *Hemerocallis longituba*. The flowers had a long perianth tube, and their the color was supposed to be fulvous.

Hemerocallis fulva angustifolia Baker. A daylily that was considered to belong with the species *H. fulva* was described under the varietal name *angustifolia* in 1871 by Baker. He describes his plants as very small with scapes scarcely 1 ft. tall, and with leaves only 12–18 in. long and only 2–4 in. wide. The segments of the flowers are described as narrow and acute; but there is no definite mention of color. It is of special interest to note that this description was based on dried specimens which, it is stated, came from Khasia, India; Guriev, which is near the extreme northwestern side of the Caspian Sea; and from Karabagh, which is farther south and in Caucasia. It seems that this form with narrow leaves may be related to one of the types recently described as *H. forrestii, H. nana,* or *H. plicata* or that it may belong with a new species. At least Baker's plants may be disregarded as a type to be included with *H. fulva* of Linnaeus or as closely related to it.

H. fulva longituba Maximowicz. The Russian botanist Maximowicz described in 1885 and illustrated with a colored plate certain daylilies of a type obtained from the wild in the Hakone Mountains of Japan and said also to be in cultivation in Japan. The flowers are described as orange-yellow with slight fulvous tinges and as having a long and narrow perianth tube. This type is described as different from the *H. fulva* of Linnaeus (the clone 'Europa') in having narrower leaves and also flowers with less fulvous color and a longer perianth tube. The description by Maximowicz is followed by a note by E. Regel, Director of the Botanical Garden in St. Petersburg, stating that in good garden soil these wild plants differ from the old form of *H. fulva* chiefly in having a long perianth tube.

Hemerocallis fulva clone 'Maculata'. The clone 'Maculata' is similar to the Europa Daylily. The coloring of the flowers is only slightly different; the fulvous shades in the outer half of the opened flower are slightly paler, and the arching band across the mid-section of the petals is slightly darker. The flowers are larger than those of the Europa Daylily and the petals are of a different shape. The period of blooming is somewhat later, but they are very similar in habit of growth except that the scapes are slightly shorter. All the plants of this clone are self-sterile, so they set no seed from pollination among themselves. They are also triploid and decidedly sterile, but have been utilized in hybridization.

In 1903 Sprenger reported that he had obtained hybrids with *H. fulva* clone 'Maculata' as a pollen parent on *H. citrina* and on *H. aurantiaca* clone 'Major'.

Hemerocallis fulva clone 'Hupehensis'. This clone was derived from a seedling plant grown by C. Sprenger in Naples, Italy from a seed collected by Padre Cypriani in Hupeh, China. The first published mention of this clone appeared in 1906 when the flower was described as "reflexed, undulating, bright coppery red, with yellow throat."

Hemerocallis fulva clone 'Cypriani'. This clone has the same source and history as clone 'Hupehensis'. Willy Muller described the flowers as "coppery red with a golden center and a well marked golden line down the middle of the petals. The form is gracefully reflexed." This and the clone 'Hupehensis' are fulvous daylilies very similar to various wild seedlings which the writer has grown. They have no special merit as garden plants.

Fulvous Daylilies in the Literature of Oriental Plants

Various botanical treatments by Japanese botanists and by Europeans who have observed or collected plants in Japan and China make mention of fulvous daylilies. In some cases the single-flowered types of the fulvous daylilies, other than the *H. aurantiaca* which will be discussed later, are included in the name *Hemerocallis fulva*, but are by some writers all called *H. disticha*, while in a few instances reference is made to *H. fulva* var. *longituba*.

In none of these descriptions and lists is there a critical discussion of the types and variations that were observed, nor are adequate descriptions and comparisons of the cultivated and the wild types made.

Fulvous daylilies of wild origin have been obtained from various localities in Japan and China and grown at The New York Botanical Garden. All these plants are very much alike in general habit of growth. The leaves are light green, medium coarse, strongly distichous, and ascending-curving. The scapes stand at a height of about 4 ft. Compared with the Europa Daylily they have foliage that is usually less robust. Some have shorter scapes, while others have taller scapes. They all, however, possess the same feature of spreading rhizomes, and the capsules are of the same type.

There is much variation in respect to the precise character of the flowers of these plants. All have some shade or degree of fulvous red in the coloring of the face of the flower, and in most cases there is a somewhat darker zone just outside of the throat of the flower. Some of the plants from Japan have duller and more brownish shades; some of those from Kuling, China have bright shades of pink and red, and to this type the varietal name *Hemerocallis fulva* var. *rosea* has been given. Many of the latter bear flowers having a long perinanth tube, and the segments are long and narrow, for which type the most proper botanical name is *H. fulva* var. *longituba* Maxim.

Several groups of fulvous daylilies obtained from Korea and northern Japan are taller and more robust than the Europa Daylily and bloom later in summer. One group has continued in flower from August until severe killing temperatures occur in November.

Possibly a more complete knowledge of the natural distribution of the various types of fulvous daylilies will reveal that there are really two or more distinct species which are more or less intermingled and which have hybridized in some overlapping areas. At the present time it seems best to include the variations, both of the wild and of the cultivated plants discussed above, in the one species *H. fulva* L., of which the clone 'Europa' is the historical type.

Hemerocallis aurantiaca Baker

Orange-Fulvous Daylily. The name *Hemerocallis aurantiaca* was given by Baker in 1890 to a plant that was then growing in the Royal Botanic Gardens at Kew, England. The origin of this plant was not definitely known except that it was believed to have been received from Japan. It was propagated by division leading to a clone of plants now in cultivation in Europe and North America under the name *H. aurantiaca. Somoku-Dzusetsu*, an early Japanese treatise on plants, includes a picture of a daylily which was said to grow wild in the region of Mt. Ibuki, and which was later considered by Makino to depict *H. aurantiaca*. It is, however, not certain that the clone described by Baker is typical of a wild type that exists in Japan. Baker's plant may even be of horticultural origin.

The plant stands with scapes about 3 ft. high, extending well above the mound of leaves. The foliage is medium coarse, strongly distichous, stiffly recurving, and decidedly evergreen in that it remains green and growing until winter comes. These clusters of leaves suffer somewhat from winter injury, but with the coming of warm weather in spring the plant soon recovers and so can be classed as hardy at about New York City. In the tropics this daylily and certain of its hybrids remain green and growing throughout the year. The scapes are coarse, ascending rather than erect, coarsely branched above, and with nodes without branches which bear conspicuous leaflike bracts. The flowers are either sessile or on short, stout pedicels. The open flower has a spread of about 5 in. The segments are stiffly recurving, of firm texture, and those on the lower side of the flower are less recurving, giving to a flower the appearance of being less widely open than flowers of other species excepting those of *H. dumortierii*. In the throat the color of the flower is orange, but outside of this area the petals and sepals are delicately tinged with English red, and hence this type is to be classed as a fulvous daylily. It is, however, very distinct from the various types of *H. fulva*. Its scapes are lower; the foliage is darker green and more evergreen; the flowers are only pale fulvous, without reticulations, less widely open and segments are narrower. The season of bloom is in July at the time when the Europa Daylily is in flower.

The so-called *H. aurantiaca major* is very similar to *H. aurantiaca* in habit of growth, character of foliage and scapes, and season of flowering so the identity of the two is sometimes confused in horticultural literature, but the flowers of the latter are much larger, have no trace of fulvous coloring, and the plant is less hardy.

Hemerocallis exaltata Stout

This species has recently be described from living plants obtained through the kindness of Mr. T. Susa and collected wild on the Tobi Shima Islands off the west coast of

Japan. The plant is robust, the mound of coarse foliage reaching a height of about 30 in. and the scapes 4–5 ft. The crown is compact without spreading rhizomes. The main roots are mostly slender-cylindrical but a few are somewhat enlarged. The scapes are stiffly erect, with coarse short branches at the extreme top. The flowers are light orange in color, spreading to a width of about 4 in., rather full, the petals somewhat spatulate in shape, and widely open during daylight hours. The period of flowering is late June and July. The capsules are elliptic in outline, as much as 1½ in. long, and noticeably corrugated with numerous, short ridges.

Hemerocallis exaltata is readily distinguished from the other species of daylilies. Its flowers and capsules resemble those of H. middendorffii but the plant is much more robust and the scapes are decidedly branched, although the branches are rather short and coarse.

The Many-Flowered Daylily

Hemerocallis multiflora Stout

This daylily was first described in 1929 from living plants found growing wild at Ki Kung Shan, Honan, China by Dr. Albert N. Steward and sent by him to The New York Botanical Garden. The crown branches are compact without spreading rhizomes. The roots are fleshy with rather short enlargements. The foliage is ascending-arching to a general level of about 20 in., is medium fine, and dies in late autumn after freezing temperatures but remains erect for a time, changing to shades of brown. The scapes are slender, in most plants ascending-bending, much and finely branched, and bearing throughout the entire season of bloom numerous flowers. The flowers are spreading to a width of about 3 in., a shade of orange that approaches "chrome," the perianth tube is tinged with green, and the back of the sepals is slightly brownish red. Two of the plants originally obtained from China bloom during July and August but the others flower from late in August until heavy freezing temperatures occur, sometimes as late as November. The capsules are seldom more than 1 in. in length and ovoid or obovoid in shape, but with relatively large seed.

H. multiflora. Photo by SIGEL

Hemerocallis dumortierii Morren

Dumortier's Daylily is one of the earliest of daylilies to bloom in spring. The plants usually stand less than 2 ft. tall. The stems branch compactly in the crown and spreading rhizomes are lacking. The roots are conspicuously enlarged. The foliage is rather stiffly ascending-spreading and the leaves are 1 in. in width, appearing somewhat coarse for the stature of the plant. The scapes are unbranched, slender, usually shorter than the leaves, not erect but merely ascending at an angle, and mostly disposed around the periphery of the mound of foliage. The flowers are sessile or on short pedicles, with usually 2–4 flowers compacted into close inflorescence with overlapping basal bracts of which the lowest is nearly 2 in. in length and accuminate. The flower buds are strongly tinged with brownish red which persists on the back of the sepals after the flower is open. The petals are about 2 in. long and ½ in. in greatest width; the sepals are smaller, and in opening the segments are merely spreading and not recurving, hence the flower is not widely open. The color of the flower's inner surface is orange without any trace of fulvous tints. The capsules when well-formed are at least 1 in. in length and decidedly globose in shape.

Living plants of *H. dumortierii* were sent by M. von Siebold from Japan to the Botanical Garden at Ghent where they first flowered in 1832.

Several clones in cultivation under the names *H. rutilens, H. sieboldii,* and even *H. minor* must be included in the species *H. dumortierii* or as somewhat aberrant forms of it. Some of these are not more than 1 ft. in height so are classed as truly dwarf. Whether these have originated from cultivated types or represent wild types is not known.

H. dumortierii. Photo by SIGEL

Hemerocallis middendorffii Trautvetter and Meyer

The first mention of Middendorff's Daylily, or the Amur Daylily, was published in 1856 and referred to herbarium specimens collected by the botanist Middendorff in the Amur Region. Ten years later living plants of this species were being grown in the Royal Botanic Garden at St. Petersburg. Plants of this daylily grow compactly in the crown and lack spreading rhizomes, the roots being cylindrical, fibrous, and not fleshy. The foliage is medium dark green in color, seldom more than 2 ft. long or more than ¾ in. in width. The scapes are unbranched, rather upright, and slightly taller than the foliage. The flowers are closely clustered at the apex of the unbranched scape, with the lower part almost enclosed in a broad bract that is rather short and blunt. The flower bud is decidedly ridged or pleated. The flower opens widely to a spread of about 3 in.; the petals are noticeably spatulate in shape, and the color is a uniform orange. The capsules are triangular in cross-section and elliptic in longitudinal outline, somewhat similar in general shape to the capsules of *H. flava* and *H. minor*, but the surface is more or less corrugated with lateral ridges.

Wild plants have been obtained from Japan which are probably of this species but differ somewhat from the older type in culture. Some have slightly paler flowers; some have taller and more erect scapes more like the *H. middendorffii major*; for some the flowers number as many as 10 to a scape, and at least some of the flowers have a distinct pedicel.

H. middendorffii major is somewhat more robust and the flowers more numerous on a scape, but otherwise it is almost identical to the type described above.

H. middendorffi. Photo by SIGEL

Species Identified and/or Described by Dr. Hu

Hemerocallis altissima Stout

Plant with medium-course, ascending-spreading leaves. Roots coarsely fibrous, few, with slight spindle-shaped enlargements. Pseudobu
erect, rhizomes short. Leaves 2–4 ft. long, ¾–1 in. wide, wiry in autumn, over-winter in a conspicuous mound. Scapes 4–6½ ft. tall, stiff, erect, branched in the upper 1/4–1/5; bracts foliaceous, the lowest 2½–4 in. long, becoming brown when first flowers open, falling off later. Flowers July–September, nocturnal, fragrant, inception of flowering 3:00–5:00 P.M., fully open 5:00–9:00 P.M., end of flowering 5:00–8:00 A.M., pale yellow, trumpet-shaped, 3 in. in diameter; the tube 1½–2 in. long; perianth-segments 2¾–4 in. long. Capsules widest at summit, immature ones ⅞ in. long, ¾ in. in diameter.

H. altissima. Photo by SIGEL

Hemerocallis coreana Nakai

Roots horizontally rugose. Leaves 5–17 in. long, ¼–½ in. wide. Scapes 20–32 in. tall, apical end branched; lower bracts lanceolate, 4–12 in. long, upper ones ovate. Flowers subsessile, perianth yellow; tube 1–2 in. long, yellowish green, segments 2½–3 in. long; the outer ½ in. wide. Capsules ca. 1 in. long, ¼ in. across, rugose, nervose, apical end emarginate.

Hemerocallis esculenta Koidzumi

Roots enlarged throughout, with no obvious tubers. Leaves 8–13 to a ramet, 20–33 in. long, ¾–1¼ in. wide, arching, minutely papillate along the margin. Scapes erect 25–35 in. tall; bracts often occur above the first branching of the inflorescence, membranous, 1 in. long; flowers 5–6, trumpet-shaped, in two abbreviated branches; pedicels ¼–¾ in. long, subtended by ovate-lanceolate bracts ¼ in. long; perianth orange, 3¼–4 in. long, tube ¾–1 in. long, segments 2¾–3¼ in. long, the outer 1¼ in. wide, the inner 1¾ in. wide. Capsules oblong, about 1 in. long, truncate and notched at the rounded tip. Seeds ovoid, ca. ¼ in. in diameter.

Hemerocallis graminea Andrews

Plants of dwarf habit. Leaves about 30 in. long, linear, keeled, grasslike. Scape as long as the leaves, bending, bearing 2–3 flowers; bracts lanceolate, 2 in. long, brown after flowering. Flowers large, 4 ½ in. across, lasting 2–3 days; buds green with a brown tint; tube short and stout; segments broad, recurving, orange with a yellow throat, browning outside, the outer ¾ in. wide, the inner 1 in. wide, margin wavy.

Hemerocallis hakunensis Nakai

Leaves short, keeled, 25–30 in. long, ⅜–⅝ in. wide. Scapes 34–40 in. tall, branched, bearing 6–11 flowers; axis of the branches 3–5 in. long, bracts ovate ½–1¼ in. long. Flowers orange, tube ⅞–1 in. long; segments 2½–3 in. long, ½–⅝ in. wide. Capsules broadly ellipsoid, 1 in. long, ¾ in. in diameter, the tip with three elevated lobes, horizontally roughened.

H. hakunensis. Photo by SIGEL   *H. hakunensis.* Photo by SIGEL

Hemerocallis littorea Makino

Roots spindle-shaped. Rhizomes elongated, light yellow. Leaves deep green, 35 in. long, 13/16 in. wide, smooth, firm, with several elevated nerves. Scapes stout, bearing proliferations in the axils of bracts, branched at the tips; bracts ovate to narrowly deltoid-ovate, the lower ones 2 in. long, lanceolate. Flowers few to many, subsessile or with short pedicels about 3/8 in. long; perianth dark orange-red or orange-yellow, 3½–5 in. long, wide-spreading; tube 5/8–1¼ in. long; inner segments broad lanceolate, recurving, 13/16 in. wide, with dark brown eye zone and light mediam longitudinal lines, margin membranous. Capsules oblong, 13/16–1⅛ in. long, horizontally ribbed.

Hemerocallis micrantha Nakai

Leaves 34 in. long, 1¼ in. wide. Scapes above the foliage, branched near tip, the branches forked, 4 flowered; bracts ovate, long-attenuate, the lower ones 3 in. long, lanceolate. Flowers orange; tube ⅞ in. long, ⅛ in. thick; segments oblanceolate, 1½ in. long, ¼ in. wide, obtuse at the tip.

Hemerocallis pedicellata Nakai

Leaves 30–35 in. long, ⅜–¾ in. wide. Scape 25 in. tall, 5/16 in. in diameter; bracts lanceolate or ovate, 13/16–1¼ in. long, membranous; pedicels 13/16–1 13/16 in. long. Flowers red-orange; tube 13/16–1 in. long, segments lanceolate, 3-5/16–3¾ in. long.

2

Breeders: Yesterday, Today and Tomorrow

Breeding of Daylilies

The breeding of daylilies is a relatively new development emerging over the past 85 years with little or no activity prior to the turn of the century. Daylilies had been introduced into Europe by explorers traveling overland routes from the Orient to Europe or over sea routes via Lisbon, Portugal. These plants had been accepted and admired-but little interest in "improving" them through hybridization was evident. Breeding started quite slowly but has recently reached a fever pitch with literally hundreds of people making crosses and registering cultivars with the American Hemerocallis Society. It is estimated that between 100,000 and 250,000 new daylily seedlings are being grown annually in the United States alone.

There is no way to capture the significant contribution that a host of nonprofessional—"backyard"—hybridizers have made on the development of daylilies. Between 1945 and 1957 when the first daylily checklist of named cultivars was compiled there were over 250 people breeding, introducing and/or selling daylilies, a significant number since the first known breeding program had only been established in the mid 1850s by Amos Perry, Enfield, Middlesex, England. Today that number has doubled! And because so many have been involved it is impossible not only to assess a particular individual's impact, but even to judge the plants created or to follow any heritage that could relate or be traced to the species or early hybrids. I will not attempt to list all breeders or breeders' programs but will identify or describe specifically these breeding programs known first-hand—or those which in the author's opinion have had a major impact upon the daylily we know today. But I do acknowledge the significant contribution made by all who have worked with daylilies from the beginning. Since interest in daylilies has increased so rapidly, in sort of a geometric progression, it is difficult to comprehend much less understand and certainly unwise to assert that any one breeder has made the greatest progress or the greatest contribution. But over the years certain breeders and their programs seem to rise to the top and therefore warrant special recognition. It is to these titans I wish to pay homage by giving special notice or recognition for what they achieved.

I have chosen to divide the "Breeding Years", as I call them, into three eras: The Early Years, 1900–1950; The Middle Years, 1950–1975; The Present and Future Years, 1975–1995. These periods have no specific relationship to special events or historical landmarks. However, they do seem to relate to time periods associated with certain breeders, their programs and the impact they have had on subsequent breeders.

The Early Years, 1900–1950

The foremost breeder and collector of daylilies in the United States during this period was Arlow Burdette Stout. His love affair with daylilies began in the 1920s while he was Director of the New York Botanical Garden. He produced his first cultivar 'Mikado' in 1929. It was first offered for sale by The Farr Nursery Company of Weiser Park, Womelsdorf, Pennsylvania.

Other cultivars were to follow:

'Wau-Bun'–1929, a twisted, pale yellow.
'Bijou'–1932, a small orange.
'Taruga'–1933, a lemon, spider type.
'Chengtu'–1935, an orange and red blend. A selected clone of *H. fulva,* from China.
'Dauntless'–1935, a buffy cream-yellow.
'Patricia'–1935, a cream-lemon.
'Aladdin'–1941, a gold with brown eye.
'Autumn Prince'–1941, a late, yellow-gold.
'Baronet'–1941, a copper-red.
'Brunette'–1941, a black-purple.
'Caballero'–1941, a rose and yellow bicolor.
'Dominion'–1941, a dark red.
'Sachem'–1941, a red-black.
'Theron'–1941, a wine-purple.

Dr. Stout was not only a collector, grower, breeder, and scientist but also the author of the first and perhaps still most definitive work on daylily species. The work has just been reprinted and remains the standard that others are measured by. It has withstood the test of time, and although questions are now emerging, extensive collecting, growing and evaluation must go forward before any significant modifications are warranted. His approach was experimental and included all forms of daylilies (species and hybrids), but with a special interest directed to red coloration, late-flowering cultivars and *H. altissima* (1942), a species from China with a great potential for breeding tall-growing cultivars suitable for the garden. His interest in very late cultivars that prolonged the season was exemplified by 'Autumn Prince'. His work on collecting and disseminating as well as hybridizing provided the foundation for future breeding programs to build upon, especially in the United States.

Two English plantsmen began work with daylilies about the turn of the century or before. They were George Yeld and Amos Perry and each was to have a marked impression on the development of daylilies. But because of plant dissemination problems, they never had the impact that they should have had in North America. Though these two English breeding programs emerged many years prior to the renaissance of daylilies in America, work in the States in the early '40s and '50s was soon to eclipse their early and masterful beginning.

George Yeld, a schoolmaster, lived from 1845 to 1938 in Gerrald's Cross, England and became a leading breeder of daylilies and iris. He named 'J. S. Gayner' in 1928. It was introduced in 1930 by Maurice Prichard & Sons, Ltd., Riverslea Nursery, Christchurch, Hants, England. 'J. S. Gayner' was an extremely fine, early, orange-yellow cultivar and was heavily used by many breeders in the United States in the late '40s and '50s.

Amos Perry lived from 1871 to 1953 in Enfield, Middlesex, England. He was founder of Perry's Hardy Plant Farm and a breeder of many hardy plants, including over 300 daylilies.

Some of these were:

'Alba Striata'–1934.
'Bradley'–1946.

'Byng of Vimy'–1936.
'Exeter'–(1938) 1946.

As the work of Yeld and Stout became better known and their plants disseminated, interest in daylilies began to grow and expand. During this period there emerged several distinctive breeding programs that were to have major impact on daylilies and their transformation from a generally utilitarian landscape plant to one of unique and uncommon beauty. Leaders in this transformation were Ralph Wheeler, Ophelia Taylor and Elizabeth (Betty) Nesmith.

It was my good fortune to know Ralph W. Wheeler in the late 1940s and early 1950s. His planting of daylilies was in Winter Park, Florida in a low lying, sandy, marshlike area. He began his work in the late 30s and by the '40s had produced a series of very special and unique cultivars.

Ralph Wheeler's interest was directed to the new, different and unique—particularity as related to form. He had an incredibly discerning eye for the unique and the special. He was one of the few breeders I knew who practiced the art of mixing pollen which he spread with a sable brush. It is obvious that the "scientist" in all of us objects to not knowing the parentage of a cultivar and what influence a specific cultivar could have. Still, the achievements of this man immediately set standards that would dictate our perception of daylilies and what they could be.

Some of his achievements were:
'Amherst'–1946, purple.
'Asia'–1948, voluptuous, gold and pink beige blend.
'Bobolink'–1946, purple and cream small bicolor.
'Brackel'–1943, brown.
'Cellini'–1949, flat, round, form lemon-yellow.
'Easter Morn'–1944, round, buff pink-yellow.
'Ganymede'–1947, magenta.
'Madam Butterfly'–1950, large orange with brown eye.
'Naranja'–1948, rich orange.
'Psyche'–1950, large ruffled and fluted cream with pinkish eye.
'Raven'–1951, black-red.
'Scarlet Sunset–1947, early, brilliant scarlet.
'Scorpio'–1952, large, yellow-gold spider.
'Show Girl–1951, lavender, of round exceptional form.

Florida was to produce another breeder of major significance in the early '40s. Mrs. Bright (Ophelia) Taylor. Ophelia was a gardener and grower of daylilies who had fame thrust upon her. In the early part of the '40s she was to grow a seedling from a cross she believed to be *H. aurantiaca major* × *H. fulva rosea* f2. It was named 'Prima Donna' and introduced in 1946. This cultivar became the foundation for her most significant work. One can not be totally sure that the cross is accurate, but based upon knowledge of *H. aurantiaca major* and *fulva rosea* and their various offspring, it appears very plausible. And considering the material she had in her garden to work with one becomes more comfortable with the hypothesis.

'Prima Donna' rose in the ranks of the then daylily world to win all awards. It was also an easy and productive parent, producing lush, large, wide, full pastels in hues not previously seen in daylilies. The pastel, multi-blended daylily had arrived. 'Prima Donna' was to leave her mark, not only in a visual way, but as an evergreen daylily with a tendency to be somewhat tender in some of the coldest locations, and whose progeny apparently possessed the same tendency. Still beauty can strike one blind to "libelous traits," and I vividly recall the incredible beauty of 'Sugar Cane', a honey-cream, pastel cultivar of very broad voluptuous form. The beauty the future was to hold was mirrored in that early cultivar. It was a memorable moment for me, as a young novice, developing an interest in this incredible perennial.

Some of her other special, early creations were:

'Cluny Brown'–1946, brown and yellow bicolor.
'Lochinvar'–1947, copper-red.
'Lodestar'–1950, buff and pink, star pastel.
'Nantahala'–1954, cream-yellow with violet eye.
'Sally O'Neal'–1948, flamboyant lemon-yellow.
'San Francisco'–1949, creamy orange with tan eye.
'Sunset Sky'–1952, rose-red potpourri stippled on cream.

No account of breeders in the early years would be complete without the mention of the work of Mrs. Thomas (Elizabeth) Nesmith. Known as Miss Betty, her breeding program and her Fairmount Gardens were synonymous with quality. She was most interested in color and experimented extensively with pinks, reds and purples. Her 'Sweetbriar' introduced in 1938 heralded the beginning of pink coloration in daylilies. Twelve years later she was to introduce 'Pink Prelude', a true milestone in style and pink color. Compared to today's cultivars it is of course muddy, "fulvasy" and poorly formed. But it was a beginning and became a trend setter.

In 1942 she was to introduce 'Potentate', a violet-plum which along with Ralph Wheeler's 'Amherst' and A. B. Stout's 'Theron', was to be the foundation of most lavender and purple breeding programs for the next 15 years.

'Royal Ruby' introduced in 1942 was as important to future red programs as 'Potentate' was to purple. Where Ophelia Taylor placed emphasis on form and style, Betty Nesmith placed emphasis on color clarity and plant refinements. These two women were remarkably similar, each with an uncanny eye for selection and an intuitive breeding talent; each producing major advances in daylilies and at a time when the only material available was very primitive and just a step or two from the species.

Few records are available regarding the heritage of their hybrids. It is remarkable enough to find even a few records of the various crosses these two pioneers made—neither were scientists nor plantsmen and record keeping was not viewed as being terribly important! And though both kept some records, neither saw the need for them.

During the late '40s and early '50s three extremely important breeders with small but significant programs emerged. Each pursued a separate and diverse program and each had significant impact on the daylilies of the day. They were Hooper P. Connell, Baton Rouge, Louisiana; Mrs. Hugh W. (Mary) Lester, Atlanta, Georgia; and Carl S. Milliken, Arcadia, California. Some of their cultivars are listed below.

Hooper P. Connell:	'Limoges'–1952, light yellow polychrome.
	'Marse Connell'–1952, dark red self.
	'Mentone'–1956, pale old-rose self.
Mary Lester:	'Maid Marian'–1950, light rose.
	'Limelight'–1951, large, late, light yellow.
	'Picture'–1952, large, rose-pink.
	'Port Royal'–1953, bright orange-red.
	'Garden Sprite'–1957, apricot self.
Carl S. Milliken:	'Colonial Dame'–1948, orange-yellow.
	'Pompeian Red'–1948, orange-red.
	'Ruffled Pinafore'–1948, orange-yellow.
	'High Noon'–1949, orange-yellow.
	'Golden Galeon'–1954, deep apricot.

The Middle Years, 1950–1975

The 25 years represented here produced some of the most exciting advances in daylilies the breeders' art was to produce. In this period over 15,000 cultivars were registered with the American Hemerocallis Society. This fact alone should attest to the fever pitch that breeding had reached. Over 450 people were breeding, naming and/or selling daylilies during this period. In light of this overwhelming number any overview of the period is perhaps doomed before it is started. However, if one looks to the "giants" of the period one can sketch a sound impression of the work accomplished. It is important to recognize that cultivars which never became "stella stars" still ultimately served the cause of improving the daylily, and played a vital part in this history and the daylily's passing parade. Record keeping was poor during the early years, nor regrettably was it to improve during the middle years except in a few isolated instances.

Many of the foremost breeders of this period began their work during the period I called "the early years" but did not hit their stride or have considerable impact until the middle period.

It is difficult to select which one to discuss first so I will mention three of the period's foremost breeders and collectors together. They were: Ezra Kraus, David Hall and Elmer Claar.

DR. EZRA KRAUS

Dr. Ezra Kraus was a professor of botany and breeder of daylilies and chrysanthemums. His record keeping was exemplary and his program very complex and expansive. He grew many seed from a single cross to study the subtle variations and any dramatic mutations that might occur. He used many numbered seedlings repeatedly in his carefully planned program in search of the unique and the beautiful. He studied the results of the numbered seedlings he crossed as carefully as he studied his structured breeding programs based on named cultivars. His work reflects a desire for perfection—and quality at all cost. His untimely death cut short a very impressive and productive career. He named hundreds of cultivars, but a few that set new standards in breeding daylilies are:

'Allegra'–1952, light yellow self, ('Crawford' × 'J. S. Gayner').

'Autumn Daffodil'–1951, light yellow self, [('Sunny Morn' × 'Dominion' × 'Gypsy') × ('Amaryllis' × 'Golden West')].

'Biretta'–1956, ruby-red self, ['Mabel Fuller' × ('Cressida' × 'Rajah')].

'Black Leopard'–1953, patterned dark red, ('Dominion' × 'Romany Lass').

'Calumet'–1952, medium yellow-orange self, ('Rosalinda' × 'Joanna Hutchins').

'Chetco'–1956, medium Chinese-yellow self, ('Double Value' × 'Maitou').

'Evelyn Claar'–1950, light red self. Parentage unknown.

'Flambeau'–1950, medium orange-red self, [('Wau-Bun' × 'Rajah') × ('Rajah' × 'J. S. Gayner')].

'Mabel Fuller'–1950, medium orange-red self, {['J. S. Gayner' × ('J. S. Gayner' × 'Gypsy')] × ('Dominion' × 'Cressida')}.

'Multnomah'–1954, apricot blend overlaid with pink, (Seedling #5076 × 'Ruth Lehman').

'Red Dot'–1950, orange-red with a dark eye, {['Rajah' × ('Bijou' × Dominion')] × ('J. S. Gayner' × 'Rajah')}

'Ringlets'–1950, orange-yellow self, {[('Mrs. W. H. Wyman' × Rosalinda') × ('Dominion' × 'J. S. Gayner')] × ('Dominion' × 'Cinnabar')}

'Rhodora'–1952, light ruby red, third generation ['Gypsy' × ('Amaryllis' × 'Dauntless')].

'Ruth Lehman'–1951, patterned light orange-red, {('Gypsy' × 'J. S. Gayner') × [('Amaryllis' × 'Golden West') × 'Gypsy']}.

'Vermilion Cliffs'–1948, medium orange-red self, ('Dauntless' × *H. fulva rosea*), the latter near vermilion-red that was heavily used in breeding.

DAVID F. HALL

During this period a breeder of *Iris*, named David F. Hall, turned his attention to the task of improving the daylily. He was a lawyer living in Wilmette, Illinois and could be described as an amateur, backyard breeder but his work was anything but amateurish. His love for the clear bright colors of *Iris* inspired and spurred him to try to create daylilies in similar colors. He was to establish two major line-breeding programs, one in pink and one in red, which forever changed the face of the modern daylily and how we would look at them. He was to be the first who truly unlocked the color pink and rose in daylily.

The Gilbert H. Wild Nursery Company of Sarcoxie, Missouri bought the rights to the Hall cultivars in 1950, but Hall continued to build upon these early lines and orchestrated the continued development of the Hall lines until 1975 by traveling to Sarcoxie during the bloom season each year and carrying on his work there.

Some of his premier achievements during these periods were:

'Coral Mist'–1955, shell pink self, 4th generation line breeding from ('Mission Bells' × *H. fulva rosea*).

'Fascination'–1948, medium yellow. Parentage unknown.

'Hearts Desire'–1951, light red-violet, 3rd generation line breeding from [('Mission Bells' × *H. fulva rosea*) × 'Evelyn Claar'].

'Magic Dawn'–1956, rose pink self. Parentage unknown.

'May Hall'–1957, pink blend. Parentage unknown.

'Maytime'–1955, pink self. Parentage unknown.

'Peach Brocade'–1957, pink self. Parentage unknown.

'Peach Chiffon'–1955, peach-pink. Parentage unknown.

'Persian Rose'–1955, rose-pink blend. Parentage unknown.

'Pinafore'–1955, salmon-pink self. Parentage unknown.

'Pink Brocade'–1955, blend of pink. Parentage unknown.

'Pink Frills'–1955, blend of pink. Parentage unknown.

'Pink Orchid'–1956, salmon-peach and shell-pink. Parentage unknown.

'Pink Parade'–1955, pink blend. Parentage unknown.

'Premier'–1956, red. Parentage unknown.

'Shining Plumage'–1957, bright red self. Parentage unknown.

'War Eagle'–1957, dark red self. Parentage unknown.

ELMER A. CLAAR

Elmer A. Claar was a Chicago businessman, active in construction and management of real estate and hotel projects, who carried on his modest hybridizing program at his home on Thornwood Lane in Northfield, Illinois. He grew a limited number of seedlings but achieved the most spectacular success by creating the broadest, most creped and ruffled yellows and most brilliant, rich, broad-petaled reds of any breeder of this period. It is regrettable that the parentage of 'Alan', his first major red breakthrough which was created in the late '40s or early '50s and registered in 1953, is unknown. Some of his premier creations were: 'Sail On', 'Red Siren', 'Lexington', 'President Rice', and 'President Marcue'. His reds have affected more red breeding programs and led more breeders to work for red than any red cultivars in the history of daylilies.

Some of his earliest cultivars were:

'Chinese Laquer'–1947, medium red-orange self. Parentage unknown.

'Flamingo'–1943, light red-orange. (*H. fulva rosea* × 'Serenade').

'Plum Mist'–1948, medium violet-red self. Parentage unknown.

'Royal Crown'–1950, medium red-orange. Parentage unknown.
'Twinkle Eye'–1945, light red-orange with pattern. Parentage unknown.

W. B. MacMILLAN

W. B. MacMillan of Abbeville, Louisiana began hybridizing daylilies in the early 1950s and was to emerge as the breeder who would have a greater impact in the middle years than any other breeder. I met Mr. Mac, as he was known, in 1960 at the National Daylily Convention in Florida. It was during this visit that he shared his discontent with his early work and how his plans to start afresh. His program was to be based upon a new cultivar that he had bloomed in 1962, one he called 'President Giles' and a cultivar from a [Sdlg. × ('Chetco' × 'Dorcas')]. There may have been two separate cultivars used, but the cross was definitely a second generation cross from ('Dorcas' × 'Chetco'). He bought two other cultivars that same year: 'Satin Glass' (Fay) and 'Dream Mist' (Munson), which together with 'President Giles', 'Dorcas', and 'Chetco' would be the bricks and mortar for the foundation for his new program. He crossed these five in every conceivable combination possible.

That same year he also decided he would bloom his seedlings in 9–12 months, rather than 24–36 months as was generally done by others. His superior climatic location of Abbeville, Louisiana, rich Delta soil and horticulture expertise allowed him to achieve this goal. Consequently, he produced three generations of seedlings in three years, while elsewhere three generations took 6–9 years.

His comprehensive program was to feature cultivars with low scapes, evergreen foliage, and broad, full, round, flat and ruffled flowers. His greatest success was in cream-pinks, pastels and yellow.

His typical round, ruffled form was ultimately called "the MacMillan" form and remains the form of comparison today—25 years later. A generous man, quietly proud and genuinely modest, he was to affect the daylily in so many ways he almost transcends all who came before him. It is remarkable—and regrettable—that his record keeping was minimal. He developed his own line and stayed well within it for many, many years. He was not studying options or permutations—why cultivar "A" did such and such, or cultivar "B" didn't. He was out to create beauty and leave his mark on the daylily. This he did handily—so that years after his death his standards of quality and beauty are still unchallenged.

Some of his special cultivars were:
'Charles Buckman'–1974, lavender self, green throat.
'Ethel Baker'–1968, deep rose-pink.
'Hope Diamond'–1968, near white self.
'Mary Mae Simon'–1970, cream self, green throat.
'Moment of Truth'–1971, near white self.
'President Giles'–1962, straw self, greenish yellow throat.
'Robert Way Schlumpf'–1968, near-white self.
'Ruth Bastain'–1975, lavender self, green throat.
'Sabie'–1974, golden yellow self, green throat.
'Zadie Williams'–1973, cream and pink blend, green throat.

EDNA SPALDING

Edna Spalding was an early breeder of daylilies who lived in Iowa, Louisiana. Her impact and contributions were formidable. She did not "hybridize" daylilies, for as she said, "I merely crossed them for my own pleasure." Her daylilies shared space in her vegetable garden. She was a housekeeper, gardener and flower arranger. She reminded me of an early pioneer woman with her cloth bonnet: strong, silent and with a self-sure demeanor. Since she made few or no records of her cultivars, one has had to rely on firsthand knowledge of friends over the years. Betty Nesmith was a good friend and so Edna grew several of Betty's early pinks including 'Pink Prelude' and 'Madam Recamier', and several early lavenders including 'Potentate' and 'Su Lin'. It is not unlikely that they were the foundation cultivars ultimately leading to 'Luxury Lace', 'Lavender Flight' and 'Blue Jay'.

Pink and purple were Edna's "speciality", and as she built upon the early Nesmith foundation, so MacMillan and others were to build upon hers. It is doubtful she grew more than 400–500 seedlings a year, but those she selected were first-rate for she had a magnificent eye for quality and beauty as well as a great intuitive breeding sense. Her standards were the highest. She always carried a large kitchen knife as she walked the garden, and if a new seedling displeased her or did not meet her exacting standards, out it would go cut below the crown, never more to plague her with its shortcomings. This ruthless nature enabled her to achieve the highest of standards even though she grew but a handful of new seedlings. She had a major impact in the breeding of daylilies, not only with her cultivars, but with her sharp and insightful evaluation of a plant and what was the standard quality of the day.

Cultivars of Edna Spalding that were unique and considerably ahead of their time include:

'Blue Jay'–1962, strange, bluish violet with a darker eye and yellow-green throat.

'Dorcas'–1959, salmon-coral pink.

'Edna Spalding'–1964, baby-ribbon pink self, yellow-green throat. Selected by Miss Edna, since as she said, "I don't want someone naming a poor plant for me after I'm gone!"

'Grecian Gift'–1960, salmon-pink self with green throat.

'Lavender Bubbles'–1963, lavender self, green throat.

'Lavender Flight'–1963, deep lavender self, green throat.

'Luxury Lace'–1959, pale lilac-lavender pink self with a strong green throat.

FRANK AND PEGGY CHILDS

One of the truly wonderful experiences in my life was to know and often visit Frank and Peggy Childs of Jenkinsburg, Georgia, a couple devoted to daylilies and to each other. We were contemporaries and thus faced similar conditions and opportunities in the search for a better and more exciting daylily.

I met them in the 1950s and was able to watch a small program grow and expand to include work in singles and doubles, diploids and tetraploids and every color available in daylilies. Their work was comprehensive and spanned a period of over 30 years. They rarely grew more than 5,000 seedlings a year.

Their first major breakthrough occurred with 'Pink Dream', a clear pastel pink of great holding qualities and pristine beauty, a color that was "as pink" as any daylily had been up to that time. As a husband and wife team they were exemplary; as a breeding team they complemented each other and the other's efforts. Frank emphasized pinks and yellows; Peggy worked in lavenders and purples, but each creation was "their's".

Several major milestones occurred in this garden, some of the most significant during the middle years being:

'Cathedral Bells'–1965, pastel cream-pink tetraploid with green throat.

'Catherina Woodbery'–1967, pale lilac-orchid self with green throat. Extraordinary!

'Ferris Wheel'–1957, a brown-red with gold throat and a spider flower form.

'Frankly Fabulous'–1962, melon-pink blend with green gold throat.

'Nobility'–1957, a light yellow self.

'Pink Dream'–1951, a clear pink self.

'Pink Reflection'–1959, pink and cream-pink bitone.

'Serene Madonna'–1972, cream near-white self with green throat.
'Showman'–1963, rich apricot and peach blend, fading to pink in the sun.
'Top Honors'–1976, cream-yellow self with green throat.
If Frank and Peggy Childs had created only 'Catherine Woodbery', a clear, pristine pale pinkish lavender with whitish green throat, their place in the history of daylilies would be more than secure. This milestone plant has markedly influenced many breeding programs—most notably Virginia Peck's, Steve Moldovan's and the writer's, as a converted tetraploid, rather than as a diploid.

Tetraploids

Since the middle years saw the emergence of tetraploid daylilies it is perhaps wise to discuss them here. Further justification for addressing this rather esoteric subject here provides the basis for exploring the significant tetraploid breeding programs of the middle years. Early work was begun in the '40s by Traub, Schreiner and Buck, but major hybridizing work did not begin before the late '60s with that of Arisumi, Brown, Fay, Griesbach, Marsh, Moldovan, Munson, Peck and Reckamp laying the foundations for this daylily of the future. The conflict between tetraploid and diploid breeders that emerged in the late '60s and early '70s persists today though it is doubtful that it will continue for another 20 years as understanding is reached and quality achieved. The rich color found in tetraploids; the new patterns and distinctive eyes and edges; the texture; sun resistance; the increased resistance to disease and insects; its added vigor and stamina; all these qualities assure the tetraploid daylily of its rightful place in the world of daylilies.

In the mid-to-late '50s interest began to grow in the ploidy of daylilies and the possibility of conversion of diploid daylilies to tetraploids based on increasing genetic knowledge.

All plants and animals have a basic complement of chromosomes, small bodies within the cell nucleus that carry the genes. This basic complement is known as a haploid number of chromosomes. The gametes (sex cells) of each sex carry the haploid number of chromosomes typical of a particular species. When two gametes, male and female, unite to form the zygote the latter acquires the diploid number, twice the haploid number. Most flowering plants are diploids; that is, they have two sets of chromosomes, one from each parent in each somatic cell or body. Polyploid is the word used to describe plants with three or more sets of chromosomes. A diploid has two sets; triploids have three sets; tetraploids have four sets; pentaploids have five sets; and so on. The number of sets of chromosomes may be increased either by natural or artificial means. Tetraploids can arise accidentally in the vegetative cells due to sudden cold or heat or as the result of the union of unreduced gametes in the cause of sexual reproduction. They also can be induced artificially through the use of chemicals—such as colchicine or physically by radiation.

Spontaneous chromosome doubling occurs with some frequency in nature both among cultivated and wild species. By one estimate as many as 50% of flowering plant and fern species are polyploid in some form. With the exception of a few triploids, polyploid daylilies resulting from natural processes have not been reported. In 1932 Dr. A. B. Stout described the results of a general survey of chromosome numbers in daylilies. The somatic number of 22 chromosomes (two sets) is basic for all species of daylilies, with the exception of several clones which were found to have 33 chromosomes (triploids). Gametes have 11 chromosomes (one of each kind) in diploid daylilies. Triploid gametes have an even number of sets, and consequently triploids are sterile.

In 1937 the antimetotic effect of colchicine, an alkaloid isolated from the Autumn

Crocus (*Colchicum autumnale*) was discovered. The effect of colchicine is to inhibit synthesis of tubulin, the substance that makes up the spindle fibers, which pull the duplicate sets of chromosomes apart during cell division. This discovery gave rise to extensive attempts to induce polyploidy artificially, in both ornamental and agricultural plants, using colchicine as the agent for increasing chromosome numbers. In the course of cell division in plants treated with colchicine, similar (homologous) chromosomes fail to separate, so a double set enters one daughter cell.

Much experimentation with daylilies from 1945 to 1965 was conducted with techniques to convert diploids daylilies into tetraploids. Approaches varied from treatment of the daylily crown (by cutting off the foliage and scooping out a hollow in the flesh of the crown to expose the growing tip and saturating it with colchicine); to colchicine injection with a hypodermic needle; to a method in which newly germinated seeds were soaked in colchicine and then washed in a bath of clear water. The strength of the colchicine varied with each method as did the exposure time. Success was not guaranteed and identification of tetraploid material after treating and flowering was difficult! A further frustration arose when in many cases colchicine treatment led to the production of a chimera (a mosaic plant with both tetraploid and diploid tissue) rather then a complete tetraploid.

The work and effort required to convert plants was tedious and often frustrating so it is little wonder that few hybridizers openly embraced the concept or altered their own breeding programs. But conversion was only half the problem, for the induced tetraploid lacked the fertility common at the diploid level. Seed production at best was not easy.

It is, therefore, not difficult to understand why tetraploid daylilies were only of interest to a handful of botanists or amateur daylily breeders. Three of the earliest scientists and/or plantsmen to experiment with tetraploids were Hamilton Traub, Quinn Buck and Robert Schreiner. Each reported successful flowering of a tetraploid daylily in 1949, 1948 and 1947 respectively.

Hamilton Traub began to breed tetraploid daylilies in 1949 while working in the U.S. Department of Agriculture lab in Beltsville, Maryland, where he developed the Beltsville Series of tetraploids. He introduced the induced 'Tetra Starzynski' (1949), 'Tetra Apricot' (1951), 'Tetra Peach' (1951), and numerous others in the years following, all distributed through the U.S. Department of Agriculture. They were primitive and quite ordinary in comparison to the diploids of the day. Though the work of these three plantsmen was to begin the movement, it was not until Orville Fay and Bob Griesbach in the Chicago area and Virginia Peck and Toru Arisume, of Tennessee and Washington, D.C. respectively, developed their approaches and techniques to plant conversion that the tetraploid effort began to take hold and have some effect. During this period James Marsh, Brother Charles Reckamp, Bill Munson and Ida Munson, Frank and Peggy Childs, Steve Moldovan, Willard Barrere, Edgar Brown, Lucille Warner and Nate Rudolph also began their work.

From 1960–1965 only 17 induced tetraploids were registered, but by 1968 66 additional seedling tetraploids—i.e. cultivars from tetraploid parents—were registered. At this writing over 50 professional and amateur breeders are working with tetraploids and in excess of 5,000 tetraploid cultivars have been registered with the American Hemerocallis Society.

Why tetraploids? It is generally agreed that tetraploids have a number of advantages over diploids. Tetraploid flowers are normally larger; the colors brighter and more intense; the scapes stronger and sturdier; and the plants possess heavier substance and greater vegetative vigor. These characteristics are, in most cases, easily demonstrated when comparing a diploid control with its tetraploid version. Another major advantage lies in the greater breeding potential of tetraploids which derives from the increased number of chromosomes controlling plant characteristics. A double set of chromosomes means that each gene locus is represented four (4) times instead of two

(2) times the genetic material which in turn means that characters controlled by multiple genes, each contributing a small effect may be more intense in tetraploids.

There are 11 kinds of (different) chromosomes in *Hemerocallis*. Each kind has places (loci) for genes which control specific characters. In a diploid two alleles (forms, such as dominant or recessive) of each gene are present, while four alleles—the same or different—are present in a tetraploid.

In diploids the individual chromosomes pass at random into the gametes (pollen or egg), so each daughter cell inherits one of each of the 11 kinds which is called "independent assortment". There are valid reasons to suspect that the four homologous chromosomes in each of the 11 sets in tetraploids may not always be randomly assorted, but each tetraploid is a different case. Consequently tetraploid genetics becomes very complex, not only because twice as many chromosomes and gene loci are involved, but also because distribution of chromosomes into the gametes may differ in pattern from one tetraploid to another.

Major criticism of tetraploids hybrids in the early years centered on their coarseness; their lack of finesse, ruffling and distinction; and a lack of variety. Further, many of the early tetraploids were subject to cracking scapes in the presence of an over-abundance of water, temperature changes and/or heavy fertilization. Regardless of the breeder's perspective these allegations were entirely correct. But time and a group of dedicated hybridizers have minimized these limitations. In fact the visual qualities of tetraploids now compete very successfully with those of the very best diploids.

Of the early breeders only Virginia Peck, Brother Charles Reckamp, Steve Moldovan, Bill Barrere, Bill Munson and Ida Munson, Nate Rudolph, Lucille Warner and Jack Romine are still actively pursuing their tetraploid breeding programs. But through the years other breeders have joined their ranks and there is now a great surge in the effort to improve, refine and expand the beauty and variety of tetraploid hemerocallis. The work being accomplished today is remarkable! And there is abundant evidence that truly dramatic breaks in color, form, edging, ruffling, texture, eyes (both lighter and darker), and pattern are being realized and that major quantum leaps will soon occur leaving us breathless as to what has been obtained.

VIRGINIA PECK

Virginia Peck of Murfreesboro, Tennessee, one of today's major daylily breeders, began to work with tetraploid daylilies in the late '50s and early '60s. Her cultivars have done as much to popularize the "modern" tetraploid daylily as anyone's.

Her early work revolved around converting diploid material into tetraploid to expand the very limited tetraploid gene pool available to the early tetraploid breeders. Her work in converting the Claar reds alone—i.e., 'Sail On' and 'Red Siren'—entitle her to a significant place in daylily history.

She was a scholar and Professor of English Literature at Middle Tennessee State College, Murfreesboro during this period so the names of some of her earliest cultivars were given such unique names as 'Lusty Leland', 'Bonnie John Seton', 'Jamie Douglas', 'Douglas Dale', and 'Queen Eleanor'.

A quiet lady, self possessed and unassuming, she was sure of her program and of what she wanted to achieve. Assisted by her husband, Richard Connelly Peck, during the early years they made a formidable team. She is still actively pursuing the improvement of daylilies and continues to make major contributions to their advancement. Her major focus today is on black and white daylilies though she continues to work with reds, yellows, pinks and purples. Several of her newer near-whites are pictured in a later chapter.

The following are a few of Virginia Peck's early creations:
'Alison'—1969, pink blend, yellow throat.
'Bengaleer'—1969, deep yellow self.

'Bonnie John Seton'–1969, light yellow self, green throat.
'Cherry Chin'–1972, rose self, green throat.
'Douglas Dale'–1969, red blend, green throat.
'Earl Brand'–1968, medium yellow self, greenish yellow throat.
'Fair Annet'–1967, pink blend, cream throat.
'Flames of Fortune'–1973, melon self, flamingo throat.
'Florence Byrd'–1970, light yellow self, green throat.
'Golden Prize'–1969, gold self.
'Gypsy Laddie'–1969, rose-pink blend gold, throat.
'Heather Green'–1969, pink blend, green throat.
'Jamie Douglas'–1968, deep yellow self.
'Jock Randall'–1971, rose self, green-yellow throat.
'Jolly Pinder'–1971, red self, green throat.
'Lusty Leland'–1971, red self green-yellow throat.

JAMES MARSH

One of the truly significant breeders of the middle years was James Marsh of Chicago, Illinois. Jim was to have major impact on both diploids and tetraploids. He began his work in the 1950s and continued until his untimely death. His garden was small by any standard, but his work has withstood the test of time with lasting effect. Jim was a painter—not an artist, but he had an artist's eye. I first became acquainted with Jim in the early '60s when his 'Prairie Maid', a pale ruffled pink with a large rose eye, was taking the American Hemerocallis Society by storm. As with most significant breeders of daylilies Jim was an "amateur" breeder, a basically quiet, unassuming man and pleased with his work, but modest and unpretentious.

James Marsh's early work was with diploids, and he used the prefix "Prairie" for all of his diploid cultivars. His interest was basically in pinks, lavenders, reds and eyed varieties though he did breed minimally in other color classes. Some of his most significant diploid cultivars were:

'Prairie Blue Eyes'–1970, 5¼ in., lavender with near-blue eye zone, green throat.
'Prairie Chief'–1963, 6¼ in., red self, yellow throat.
'Prairie Dawn'–1966, 5½ in., lavender self, cream-green throat.
'Prairie Hills'–1967, 6½ in., lilac self, green-yellow throat.
'Prairie Horizon'–1967, 6 in., lavender with purple eye zone, green-cream throat.
'Prairie Maid'–1963, 5 in., melon with medium rose eye zone, green throat.
'Prairie Mist'–1962, 6 in., lavender self, pale gold throat.
'Prairie Thistle'–1963, 5½ in., light violet, cream-green throat.
'Prairie Warrior'–1963, 7 in., dark red self, green-yellow throat.

When he reached a major plateau with diploids his interest shifted to tetraploids, an interest intensified by living in the same area as Orville Fay, Robert Griesbach and Brother Charles Reckamp. His tetraploid program was to be so successful that in time it would eclipse all he had previously done. His interest in lavender and purple was all-consuming. He grew some of the most beautiful Clematis I've ever seen for which I would tease him that he only grew them as a measuring stick for evaluating his purple breeding program.

Early on Jim made a cross of 'Prairie Thistle' × 'Lavender Flight' after which he treated the newly germinated seed in an effort to convert the best of his lavender diploid line to a tretraploid. A seedling of extraordinary lavender-purple color bloomed. It was not a true tetraploid, but a chimera. In 1967 Jim crossed this major milestone with every tetraploid in his garden. Regrettably the tetraploid of this magical seedling reverted to diploid—or was somehow lost. But Jim was able to collect several hundred seed from seedling tetraploids ranging in color from cream-melon to salmon and rose, which were to be the beginning of his lavender and purple lines. He had turned a major page in daylily history. And though he would do many fine reds and a few yellows he will be remembered for his lavenders and purples. If he had done nothing but them his place in daylily history would be secure. As with his diploids Jim chose a prefix for all of this tetraploids cultivars, Chicago, and so the "Chicago" series was born.

Some of Jim's earliest tetraploids were:

'Chicago Brave'–1967, 5½ in. dark red self, green throat.
'Chicago Cardinal'–1972, 6 in., red self, green throat.
'Chicago Firecracker'–1976, 5½ in., Chinese-red self, chartreuse throat.
'Chicago Frost'–1972, 5¾ in., lavender self, green throat.
'Chicago Knobby'–1974, 6 in., purple bitone deeper center, green throat.
'Chicago Mist'–1970, 5¼in., lavender self, green throat.
'Chicago Pansy'–1977, 6 in., plum purple blend, darker eye zone, cream-green throat.
'Chicago Picotee Promise'–1976, 5½ in., purple and beige, purple eye zone, green throat.
'Chicago Picotee Queen'–1976, 6¼in., purple lavender, green throat.
'Chicago Queen'–1974, 6 in., lavender, purple eye zone, green throat.
'Chicago Regal'–1970, 7 in., purple, deeper eye zone, green throat.
'Chicago Royal'–1970, 7 in., purple bitone, green throat.
'Chicago Royal Robe'–1977, 5½in., plum-purple self, green throat.
'Chicago Ruby'–1977, 6 in., red self, green throat.
'Chicago Thistle'–1971, 5¼in., deep lavender self, pale yellow-green throat.

ORVILLE FAY

Another of the truly great breeders of the middle years was Orville W. Fay of Northbrook, Illinois. His work spanned 20 years and was exemplified by 'Frances Fay', a soft pastel, melon-cream-yellow cultivar that grew easily, multiplied well, won all A.H.S. awards and remained on the A.H.S. Popularity Poll for years. As with most breeders of daylilies, he was an amateur, his profession being that of a chemist in a candy factory until his retirement.

In 1957 and 1958 he bloomed two cultivars that would dramatically change the breeding direction of daylilies. They were 'Superfine', a large, rose-pink and 'Satin Glass', a large, cream-melon pastel. They were new plateaus in size, finish, finesse and "breeding ability".

Orville Fay was a meticulous record keeper and his results clearly show the benefit of such records.

His work was very limited in scope for he stayed in very narrow, well-defined lines. Significant cultivars were:

'Betty Rice'–1956, ['Fay 51–51' × ('Evelyn Clarr' × 'Pink Seedling') × 'True Charm'], a blend of powder-pink and lavender.
'Frances Fay'–1957, ('Fay 52–18' × 'Fay 52–30'), a pastel melon-cream self.
'Louise Russell'–1959, ('Fay 52–17' × 'Fay 52–25'), a deep baby-ribbon-pink self.
'Satin Glass'–1960, ('Betty Rice' × 'Fay 55–10'), large, voluptuous, cream-melon with green throat.
'Superfine'–1960, ('Fay 51–52' × 'Fay 52–18') a large, rose-pink-melon self.

During the '50s Orville Fay and Robert A. Griesbach embarked on a program to produce tetraploid daylilies. They introduced a technique where the newly germinated seed was soaked in a colchicine solution, washed and planted. A high percentage of the survivors were tetraploid. Mr. Fay and Dr. Griesbach introduced a group of induced tetraploids created with this method—all with the prefix of Crestwood. The most significant of these were:

'Crestwood Ann'–1961, cream-melon-pink self.

'Crestwood Gold'–1963, 6 in., gold self with green throat.

'Crestwood Evening'–1961, lemon-cream self.

Orville Fay was to produce two significant tetraploid seedlings from this induced material. They were :

'Kathleen Elise Randall'–1965, 5 in., creamy-melon with orchid midribs, green-yellow throat.

'Lady Cynthia'–1965, 5½ in., melon with pink midribs, green throat.

Both were from 'Crestwood Ann' and basically cream-pink in color, medium-size and the forerunner of a whole new breed of daylilies.

Where others sought great variety in color, size and form, Orville sought finish and refinement in the pastel melon class.

BROTHER CHARLES RECKAMP

Mission Gardens and Brother Charles Reckamp were synonymous with quality, and the work of Brother Charles with daylilies is a masterful achievement, spanning more than 30 years. I first met Brother Charles in the mid-1960s. He had already made a name for himself with diploids; however, he was soon to eclipse that work with his astounding work with tetraploids. Brother Charles was a quiet, unassuming man, yet consumed with daylilies and with a desire to improve them—and he was to fully explore this passion. His efforts were directed exclusively to pastels, ranging from near cream-white to ivory-rouged-pink and yellows, golds, apricots and oranges. His trademark, large pastels with heavily ruffled petals with gold edges, was to emerge early on.

In 1967 I visited Brother Charles and was privileged to walk the seedling fields at Mission Gardens. Tetraploids were just beginning to be known and talked about. The early work of Quinn Buck, Hamilton Traub and Orville Fay was reaching a level of true importance, but only when I saw the work of this man was I able to really understand the significance tetraploids were to have in daylilies. As far as one could see were row after row of magnificent seedlings in a large array of pastel creams, yellows and golds; stiffly erect scapes of varying heights and flowers broad and full with substance thick, heavy and waxlike. I first saw 'Holy Grail' (32 in. scape, 6 in. cream-yellow blend with a green throat) as a numbered seedling that year and it left a mark on my memory that time has not erased. Seen today and measured by today's standards it pales a bit, but for its day it was perfection, a milestone of the highest quality. A new plateau had been reached.

The cross that produced 'Holy Grail' was [(seedling × 'Betty Rice') × (seedling × 'Crestwood Ann')] × ('Bountiful Harvest' × 'Changing Times'). This very complex cross was to be the basis of much that followed. Prior to 'Holy Grail' Brother Charles had produced 'Envoy', 'Bountiful Harvest' and 'Changing Times'. All are hallmarks in that incredibly small, primitive arena of early tetraploids.

Some of Brother Charles' cultivars were:

'Little Rainbow'–1963, 2 in., melon-pink, cream, yellow and orchid polychrome with orange throat, diploid.

'Cub Scout'–1966, 3 in., apricot-gold blend with pink midribs, green throat, diploid.

'Envoy'–1966, 6 in., cream-pink blend, green-yellow throat, tetraploid.

'Changing Times'–1967, 5 in., creamy-apricot blend overlaid pink, green throat, tetraploid.

'Bountiful Harvest'–1967, 6 in., buff with orchid midribs, tetraploid.

'Bible Story'–1968, 3 in., creamy-cantaloupe-pink blend, green throat, diploid.

'Magic Wand'–1968, 6 in., apricot overlaid gold, green-gold throat, tetraploid.

'Minted Gold'–1968, 6 in., gold self, tetraploid.
'Cornerstone'–1969, 6 in., apricot-orange self, tangerine throat, tetraploid.
'Crystal Ball'–1969, 6 in., apricot-pink blend, deeper throat, tetraploid.
'Heavenly Harp'–1969, 6½in., apricot overlaid bright gold and heavy green undertones, green throat, tetraploid.
'Crown'–1970, 6 in., Canary-yellow self, green throat, tetraploid.
'Venetian Sun'–1970, 5½in., bright tangerine with pink midribs, tetraploid.
'Acolyte'–1972, 4 in., buff-cream and apricot blend, green-gold throat, tetraploid.
'King Alfred'–1975, 5½in., double, light yellow self, green throat, tetraploid.

STEVE C. MOLDOVAN

Steve Moldovan became involved with daylilies and iris as a young man and pursued a degree in ornamental horticulture. He developed Moldovan Gardens early on, stressing quality plants and distinctive beauty, and was a young protege of Orville Fay so his interest in daylilies and iris followed a similar direction. He was obsessed with parentages and has perhaps the most comprehensive "stud" book in North America today which records the crosses made by him and Orville Fay. His early work was with diploids, but he changed direction in 1961 and tetraploids became his primary concern. He has introduced cultivars developed by Orville Fay, Nathan "Nate" Rudolph, and Brother Charles Reckamp as well as his own. Moldovan Gardens is located in Avon, Ohio, a small community near Cleveland. The garden is oriental in effect with a series of garden plateaus carved out of a hillside. Broad walks, gravel areas, large stones, mugo pines, evergreen hedges and crabapples create the garden's infrastructure, the daylily beds providing the fabric that ties it all together. The garden layout has changed little over the years, but the daylily additions have become many and varied.

In 1962 he embarked on a major program to convert diploid daylilies to tetraploids using the method of treating newly germinated seedlings with colchicine. Thousands upon thousands of seedlings were treated and the resulting early conversions were the pioneers and foundation for most of his work today.

The Moldovan program has always been diverse, unique and imaginative. He quickly broke with tradition by importing many new and unique cultivars from the south, especially Florida and Louisiana, to breed with the strongly dormant cultivars of the north, particularly the cultivars of Orville Fay.

A good example of this approach in breeding can be seen in his 'Wine Merchant' (seedling #D69-25)—a cultivar of a complex heritage that is bold, imaginative and directional: [('White Jade' × seedling) × 'Blue Jay'] × ('Lavender Parade' × 'Blue Jay')] × [(seedling × 'Lavender Parade') × 'Breaking Dawn'] × [(seedling × 'Beautiful Lady') × seedling].

By crossing evergreens with dormants he was also attempting to increase the adaptability of various cultivars by making them either semievergreen or semidormant, thus broadening them to a wider geographical range of adaptability.

New colors, unique colors, clear colors were always a major goal. Purples were a passion and are exemplified by these recent magnificent creations.

'Night Town'–1984, 26 in. scape, 6 in., red-black self with lemon-green throat, early mid-season, dormant, tetraploid.
'Strutter's Ball'–1984, 28 in. scape, 6 in., black-purple with a very small, silvery white watermark above the small, lemon-green throat, mid-season, dormant, tetraploid

Each program in his breeding plan is carefully recorded, studied and orchestrated. Unlike others his seed crops are basically modest and quite limited. This is by design.

35

Some of his early cultivars were:

'Buried Treasure'–1962, 5½ in., ivory-yellow with white midribs, large green throat, diploid.

'Kwan Yin'–1967, 5½ in., pink and green blend, green throat, diploid.

'Zodiac'–1968, 5½ in., golden orange self, diploid.

'Degas'–1970, 6½ in., pink self, soft cream throat, diploid.

'Flaming Pearl'–1970, 6 in., coral-rose blend, green-yellow throat, tetraploid.

'Taipan'–1970, 4½ in., orchid-lavender blend, yellow-green throat, diploid.

'Abel'–1971, 6 in., blend of pink, orchid and lavender over cream, tetraploid.

'Adam'–1971, 5 in., red with blue cast, green throat, tetraploid.

'Eve'–1971, 6 in., pink self, green-yellow throat, tetraploid.

'Wine Merchant'–1971, 5 in., violet blend, green throat, diploid.

'Yonder Star'–1971, 6 in., ivory self, green throat, diploid.

'Imperial Guard'–1975, 5½ in., red self, yellow-green throat, tetraploid.

R. W. (BILL) MUNSON, JR.

I began to grow daylilies in 1947 and began to hybridize at once. I used cultivars from my three mentors, Ralph Wheeler, Ophelia Taylor and David Hall to start my first line. The first cross was 'Prima Donna' (Taylor) × 'Mission Bells' (Hall). Several selected seedlings were then crossed with 'Show Girl' (Wheeler) and a line of voluptuous pastel diploids followed. The line was taken to the sixth generation before I became intoxicated with tetraploids in 1960 and decided to abandon it. Significant cultivars were:

'Bridal Satin'–1959, 5½ in., voluptuous, ivory-cream, green throat.

'Dream Mist'–1958, 5 in., very full, round formed, ivory-cream rouged pink-rose, green throat.

'Hampton Court'–1966, 5 in., medium large, lavender blend, chartreuse throat.

'Incomparable'–1964, 4½ in., beautifully formed pale flesh self, cream throat.

'Jean George'–1964, 5 in., cream-flesh and pink blend, deep green throat.

'Jimmie Kilpatrick'–1964, 5 in., rose-pink blend, chartreuse throat.

'Muted Melody'–1960, 5½ in., ivory-cream-buff-pink blend, cream-green throat.

'Pickfair'–1960, 5 in., orchid pink self, cream throat.

'Sands of Time'–1957, 5½ in., honey-tan self, yellow-green throat.

'Showpiece'–1965, 7 in., yellow-gold overlaid melon, green-gold throat.

'Sleeping Beauty'–1959, 4½ in., full form, pale peach-pink self, light gold throat.

'Southern Heritage'–1958, 5½ in., exquisite full formed, pale cream and lilac blend, chartreuse throat.

'Spellbound'–1959, 5½ in., ivory washed lilac, green throat.

1960 saw the madness start and a consuming drive to develop the best possible tetraploids emerged. I obtained all the tetraploid cultivars available at that time and simultaneously embarked upon a journey to convert significant diploids by all possible methods. 1962 saw my first induced cultivar bloom. A tetraploid cultivar blending the lines of Orville Fay and Edna Spalding by crossing 'Superfine' × 'Dorcas' proved to be my first tetraploid break-through, numbered TDS-1. It became the parent along with 'Crestwood Ann' of 'Oriana', a 6 in., tomato-rose-cream with red eye zone and gold throat. 'Oriana' crossed with an induced tetraploid seedling TPMFFSB-2 produced 'Kings Cloak', a 6 in., wine-rose blend with mauve-wine eye zone and yellow-green throat. TPMFFSB-2 was an induced tetraploid from 'Prairie Mist' × ('Frances Fay' × 'Sleeping Beauty'). The same year TSGSB-100, an induced tetraploid from ('Satin Glass' × 'Sleeping Beauty'), bloomed and became a part of an elaborate foundation that 20 years later we are still building upon.

In the 1960s one searched endlessly for new tetraploid material—for the gene pool was meager and the need for more esoteric material became more obvious with each passing year. With the use of 'Crestwood Ann', 'Kathleen Elsie Randall', 'Magnifique', 'Kings Cloak', 'Tet. Chandelier Shimmer', 'Tet. Ruth Bastain', 'Astarte', 'Fugue' and 'Tet. Sari' we began to carve out our tetraploid program for today and tomorrow.

Significant early cultivars:

'Astarte'–1972, 5 in., ivory-cream-pink blend, chartreuse throat.

'Bishops Crest'–1973, 6 in., silver-mauve with purple eye band, gold throat.

'Byzantine Emperor'–1977, 6 in., burgundy with purple eye zone, yellow-green throat.

'Embassy'–1971, 6 in., raisin-red self, yellow-cream throat.

'Fugue'–1971, 5 in., orchid-pink self, cream throat.

'Kings Cloak'–1969, 6 in., wine-rose blend, mauve-wine eye zone yellow-green throat.

'Knave'–1971, 5 in., mauve-rose-red self, cream throat.

'Magnifique'–1961, 6 in., creamy-ivory tinted pink, light green throat.

'Spanish Treasure'–1969, 7 in., yellow-gold self, with yellow throat and green heart.

'Yasmin'–1969, 6 in., ivory-cream-flesh blend, chartreuse throat.

The Present and Future Years, 1976–1995

It may be presumptuous to assume that we can today predict what will happen in the future, partuculary in light of the advances of the past 75 years. And yet I feel that it is important to take the risk and identify some special cultivars that will be significant in the years from 1989 to 1995.

At no time in history has there been more people involved and work being directed toward the improvement of daylilies than there is today. The list of breeders is virtually endless. Today's breeder must come to recognize that daylilies are now both diploid (with 22 chromosomes, the count typical of the genus) and tetraploid (with 44 chromosomes, twice the count in the species or early hybrids). The unfortunate and divisive division between breeders who work exclusively with either tetraploids or diploids, or who carry on two entirely separate programs at the same time must and will come to an end in the near future.

Many of today's more successful breeders established their programs early on during the middle years. They have been part of the renaissance and continue to participate and carve new plateaus. The diploid breeders capturing most of the honors today are Elsie Spalding, Lucille Guidry, the late Charles Pierce, Pauline Henry, Elizabeth Hudson Salter, and Bob Dove (his collection recently sold to Jean Barnhart). The tetraploid breeders today capturing most of the honors are Virginia Peck, Steve Moldovan, the late James Marsh, Brother Charles Reckamp, Bill and Ida Munson, the late Edgar Brown, Harold Harris (his collection purchased by John Benz), Trudy Petree, R. L. Webster and Oscie Whatley. Significant breeders attempting to breed both tetraploids and diploids are Sarah Sikes, Kenneth Durio, Bryant Millikan and E. R. Joiner.

The interest in daylilies is spreading throughout the world. As this occurs the desire to hybridize and develop programs to improve an refine cultivars will also increase. Many such programs are getting underway. Some that have emerged recently of which I am aware are the programs in Europe and Australia.

The work in Germany has been reported in several A.H.S. publications. The overall aim or goal of most of these breeders, as I understand it, is to obtain good performance of daylilies in their climatic. This aim is the goal of most hybridizers in Europe. Lacking the warm sunshine during many of the summer months, they are all looking for varieties that will adapt to their climate conditions and still have the color and improvements achieved in the United States.

Programs of which I am aware include the work of Eckhard Berlin, Gertud Hintze, Uwe Knopnagel, Haralf Moos, the late Bruno Muller, Tomas Tamberg, and Werner Reinermann. These programs vary greatly in scope and approach. Perhaps the most active and aggressive is Werner Reinermann who apparently shifted his emphasis from iris to daylilies. He visits the United States regularly and is very knowledgeable about the work being done here.

Other programs in Europe include Stobbergs of Cologne, France; Erich Zelina of Vienna, Austria; and C. Govaerts and Francois Verhaert of Belgium.

The work in Great Britian is not well known; the death of Philip Coe brought to a close the only program of which I am aware.

Interest in daylilies in Australia is dynamic and growing; the Daylily Society of Australia was recently founded. Several programs are well underway there. Two of the best known are the Flanders/Mead program being developed by Mrs. D. J. Flanders and Mrs. C. D. Mead of Queensland, Australia. Their program has been founded upon various tetraploid cultivars essentially from the United States. A rather modest but exceptional tetraploid breeding program has been established by Barry and Lesley Blyth, Tempo Two, Pearcedale, Victoria, Australia.

As with the many programs in the United States that are just emerging, these efforts from other countries and widely varied geographical locations can only intesify the growing interest in daylilies. This interest, coupled with all the breeding expertise, will enable the genes of daylilies to adapt themselves geographically as few plants have ever done in the past.

The fact that eventually all of these breeders will continue to work until at least 1995, together with the fact that the cultivars upon which their future breeding success (as well as that of as yet unrecognized newcomers) will depend are already in existance, emboldens me to select 1995 as the closing year of this last period dealt with in the book. I have identified those breeders who by virtue of their track record will most probably continue to be in the forefront of daylily breeding for the next eight years. Now I turn to the noteworthy cultivars, all presently in existance, which will almost certainly provide the foundation for those outstanding daylilies emerging between now and 1995.

Some Worthy Daylilies of Today and Tomorrow

This section presents a listing of cultivars I feel are noteworthy irrespective of age or ploidy and are not only worthy of a place in the garden but also are the foundation for tomorrow's great daylilies. In compiling this assessment it did not seem appropriate to group today's cultivars by breeder. Rather, I thought listing them by the color classification or color categories into which daylilies are now generally grouped would be most useful to the reader. It must be pointed out that we all see color differently and that colors tend to vary from region to region and are greatly affected by sun and shade, heat and humidity, evening and night time temperatures, quantity of water, soil types and culture. The more exotic the color the more vulnerable to cultural conditions it seems to be. Generally yellow and creams are least affected while lavenders, purples and reds are most greatly affected.

The number of fine, yellow cultivars presently available greatly exceeds the number of fine purple or red cultivars. But this disparity has not influenced the number of cultivars in each color range I have chosen to include. Furthermore, I have made no effort to limit the number of cultivars in any one color class, but have included those that are, in my opinion, quite fine or very "special". It should also be noted that both tetraploid and diploid cultivars are included, and where known the ploidy of the plant is given. Singles and doubles are listed together, as well as miniature, small, medium and large.

This compilation of cultivars is based upon 40 years of knowledge and reflection gained while growing and assessing daylilies. These views have been formed not only out of a continuing assessment of my private daylily collection that exceeds 1000 named cultivars, but from repeated visits to significant gardens throughout the United States, and perhaps an overly excessive correspondence with other growers, breeders and collectors around the world. No such assessment list from any one individual can be all-inclusive and all-knowing, a fact to which I have been sensitive, so I have sought out the views of others whose judgment I respect. Since this listing is intended to encompass the leading cultivars of today and tomorrow—and since one collector, grower, breeder can not be all things to all people and in all places at once and see all cultivars—I have relied upon the "kindness of colleagues and friends" to broaden my perspective and the horizons of this work as well as to bring focus where focus was needed. I do hereby gratefully acknowledge their help, patient understanding and generous supply of advice and photographic material.

Color classification is at best ambiguous and difficult since daylilies are rarely pure "artist's" colors but are more or less blends of several shades of color overlaying a base color of some shade of yellow. The catagories selected, however imperfect, remain the best way to cope with broad ranges of colors. I have tried to avoid the use of esoteric descriptive names for colors, such as "summer" gold, "persian" apricot, etc. Gold in all its variation and gradations is for this purpose at best gold—light gold, gold, dark gold—so that is the only term generally used. There is no blue daylily, save in the breeder's eye, so I have chosen to ignore it—though work in lavender and purple is significant and heavily reported. However, the emergence of blue "tone" eyes has occurred and is worth noting.

In determining those cultivars to be included it must be noted that I have been greatly swayed by availability, adaptability, distinction and individual beauty. If a plant adapts well in several regions it is more likely to be included than one that does not. Thank goodness beauty is in the eye of the beholder so the cultivars listed herein reflect an innate beauty and distinction based upon my perception of what is "beauty" or beautiful. No more—no less.

Geographical hardiness has not been indicated since there does not seem to be any way to truly define such a characteristic for daylilies—that is, to establish guidelines having real meaning. The hardiness zones used for other perennials found in most horticultural publications are not really appropriate for daylilies, since daylilies will grow to some extent in all zones but their degree of success depends upon foliage types and plant use. Daylily foliage types range from totally evergreen through totally dormant with many gradations between these two extremes. Evergreen daylilies basically adapt best in tropical, semitropical or milder regions but do adapt to some colder regions provided a snow cover is available during the coldest periods or a winter mulch is provided. The dormant daylily is more at home in colder locations, and many times finds it difficult to adjust to short periods of cold or no cold at all. The semidormant to semievergreen cultivars, however, seem to adapt more easily to the extremes of climates than either the completely evergreen or the completely dormant cultivars.

The color classifications employed here are: Near White to Cream, Cream to Light Yellow, Yellow, Gold, Apricot-orange, Pastel cream-pink, Pink, Rose, Red, Wine, Purple, Black, Lavender, Eyed, Patterned, and Bicolored.

Eyed and patterned have not been separated into two classes but are listed together. Eyed can mean patterned but patterned does not necessarily mean eyed. It should also be pointed out that the description of each cultivar is basically a compilation of data received from several sources.

Flower size and scape height are quite variable from region to region and even garden to garden. Therefore, it seemed wise to select an average, if that is possible, and that is what I have done. It can be difficult to determine a date of introduction. Also, some cultivars listed here have not as yet been introduced, so in this work I have used the registration date of the daylily.

NEAR WHITE TO LEMON CREAM

'**Agape Love**'–1975 (W. Spalding). Semievergreen. 15 in. Midseason. Large, ruffled, 6 in., ivory-cream with pink midribs and green throat. Elegantly formed. Diploid.

'**Arctic Snow**'–1985 (Stamile). Dormant. 27 in. Early. Special, 6½ in. ruffled, flat, near white self with pale pink highlights and a pale green-lemon throat. Tetraploid.

'**Aspen**'–1981 (Millikan). Semievergreen. 24 in. Midseason. Voluptuous, 5 in., white self with green throat. Diploid.

'**At Last**'–1975 (Sellers). Semievergreen. 26 in. Midseason. 5 in., ivory-cream to near white self with green throat. Tetraploid.

'**Blanco Real**'–1978 (Harris). Semievergreen. 28 in. Early midseason. Splendid 6 in., ivory-white self with green throat. Very fine. Tetraploid.

'**Bob White**'–1982 (Peck). Dormant. 24 in. Midseason. Broad, full formed, large, 6 in., near white self with green throat. Tetraploid.

'**Call To Remembrance**'–1969 (Spalding). Semievergreen. 22 in. Early midseason. 5 in., near white self with ice pink highlights and green throat. Diploid.

'**Chablis Blanc**'–1980 (Munson). Evergreen. 28 in. Early midseason to late. Large, productive, cream self with a green throat. Has superb branching. Tetraploid.

'**Dancing Snow**'–1986 (Moldovan). Dormant. 28 in. Midseason. Pristine 5½ in., near white with pale pink and ivory highlights and a green throat. Ruffled and very full. Tetraploid.

'**Emily Jaye**'–1983 (Harris). Dormant. 29 in. Early midseason. Medium large 5 in., near white to ivory-cream with pale pink blaze and green throat. Tetraploid.

'**Gentle Shepherd**'–1980 (Yancey). Semievergreen. 29 in. Early midseason. Extraordinary 5 in., near white self with yellow-green throat. Diploid.

'**Gleber's Top Cream**'–1986 (W. Spalding). Semievergreen. 17 in. Early midseason. 6 in., extremely broad, full ivory-cream and pale pink-peach highlights with green throat. Diploid.

'**Gloria Blanca**'–1979 (Harris). Dormant. 22 in. Midseason. Large, full formed 6 in., near white self with green throat. Special. Tetraploid.

'**Jet Signal**'–1984 (Sellers). Semievergreen. 26 in. Midseason. Medium large 5 in., cream-white self with green throat. Tetraploid.

'**Joan Senior**'–1977 (Durio). Evergreen. 25 in. Early midseason. Very fine, large, 6 in., lightly ruffled, near white self with lime-green throat. Incredible vigor and production. Diploid.

'Joan Senior'. Photo by DURIO

'**Kazuq**'–1986 (Jinkerson). Evergreen. 26 in. Midseason late. 5 in. wide petaled, lightly ruffled, near cream-white with green throat. Diploid.

'Kazuq'. Photo by JINKERSON

'Lacy Bonnet'–1981 (Spalding). Semi-evergreen. 15 in. Midseason. Handsome, large, 6in., ivory-white self with green throat. Very ruffled and elegant. Diploid.

'Little Infant'–1973 (Monette). Evergreen. 20 in. Midseason. Very special, 4 in., near white-cream self with green throat. Waxy texture. A classic. Diploid.

'Moon Snow'–1983 (Munson). Evergreen. 24 in. Midseason. Handsome, medium large, 5 in., ivory-white self with cream throat. Form is broad, full, ruffled and flat. Tetraploid.

'Morning Madonna'–1979 (E. C. Brown). Evergreen. 24 in. Midseason. Beautifully formed 5 in., lightly ruffled, ivory-cream-white with chartreuse throat. Diploid.

'Morning Madonna'. Photo by BROWN, E.C.

'Munchkin Moonbeam'–1985 (Elizabeth Hudson Salter). Evergreen. 15 in. Midseason. A superb, 2½ in., ivory-cream to near white, very smooth texture and lightly ruffled edges, with lime-green throat. Diploid.

'Munchkin Moonbeam'. Photo by SALTER

'Mykonos'–1986 (Munson). Evergreen. 28 in. Midseason. Flat, lightly ruffled, 5 in., light cream to near white self with chartreuse throat. Very productive. Tetraploid.

'New Snow'–1983 (Durio). Semievergreen. 24 in. Early midseason. Special 5 in., lightly ruffled, well formed, flat, near white self with green throat and white midribs. Tetraploid.

'New Snow'. Photo by DURIO

'Pale Moon Rising'–1986 (Peck). Dormant. 23 in. Midseason. Large, 6 in., lightly ruffled and textured ivory-cream to near white with green throat. Tetraploid.

'Pale Moon Rising'. Photo by PECK

'Platinum Plus'–1987 (Peck). Dormant. 24 in., Midseason. 5 in. recurved, lightly ruffled, near white to ivory-cream with yellow-green throat. Tetraploid.

'Quietly Awesome'–1987 (Peck). Dormant. 24 in. Midseason. 6 in., broad, overlapped, lightly ruffled, near white, with green throat. Tetraploid.

'Platinum Plus'. Photo by PECK

'Ski Slope'. Photo by PECK

'Quietly Awesome'. Photo by PECK

'Snowed In'. Photo by MILLIKAN

and green highlights and a green throat. Tetraploid.

'Silver Queen'–1987 (Peck). Dormant. 23 in. Midseason. Medium large, 5 in., recurved, lightly ruffled, near white, with green-yellow throat. Tetraploid.

'Silver Queen'. Photo by PECK

'Ski Slope'–1987 (Peck). Dormant. 24 in. Midseason. Large, full and opulent 6 in., very ruffled, creped textured, cream-white, with white midribs and green throat. Wonderful. Tetraploid.

'Snowed In'–1985 (Millikan). Evergreen. 25 in. Midseason. Superb, large, voluptuous 5½ in., white, with light pink ice

'Snowy Owl'–1986 (Durio). Dormant. 24 in. Early midseason. Medium large 5½ in., near white to ivory-cream self, with light green throat. Lightly ruffled triangular form. Tetraploid.

'Swan Music'–1987 (Peck). Dormant. 23 in. Midseason. Large, 6 in., chartreuse-white to near white, recurved self, with deep green throat. Impressive. Tetraploid.

'Swan Music'. Photo by PECK

'Vail'–1984 (Millikan). Semievergreen. 25 in. Midseason. Wonderful, 5 in., near white self, with green throat. Diploid.

'**Wedding Band**'–1987 (Stamile). Dormant. 26". Midseason. Special, 5½ in., broad and full, cream to near white self, with ruffled gold edge and green throat. Tetraploid.

'Wedding Band'. Photo by STAMILE

'**White Ibis**'–1982 (Durio). Evergreen. 28 in. Early midseason. Medium large, opulent 5 in., round, recurved, diamond dusted, creamy near white self, with dark green throat. Diploid.

'White Ibis'. Photo by DURIO

'**White Minx**'–1987 (Peck). Dormant. 22 in. Midseason. Superb 5 in., round, recurved, very ruffled and fluted, near white, with chartreuse throat. Tetraploid.

'White Minx'. Photo by PECK

'**White Opal**'–1982 (Crochet). Semievergreen. 17 in. Early midseason. Very round, full formed, recurved 5½ in., near white self, with green-yellow throat. Diploid.

'White- Opal'. Photo by CROCHET

'**White Pansy**'–1987 (Peck). Dormant. 24 in. Midseason. Incredible, large, 6 in., broad petaled, flat form, textured and lightly ruffled, near white self, with white midribs and green throat. Breathtaking. Tetraploid.

'White Pansy'. Photo by PECK

'**White Temptation**'–1978 (Sellers). Semievergreen. 32 in. Midseason. 5 in., near white self, with green throat. Diploid.
'**White Tie Affair**'–1982 (Peck). Dormant. 24 in., Midseason. Very fine 6 in., near white self, with green throat. Form is broad, full, and lightly ruffled. Tetraploid.
'**Winter Olympics**'–1982 (Peck). Dormant. 20 in. Midseason. Impressive 6½ in., near white self, with green throat. Tetraploid.

'**Added Dimensions**'–1984 (Peck). Dormant. 28 in., Midseason. Large 7 in., wide and round, ruffled, medium, cream-yellow self. Cream-green-yellow throat. Tetraploid.

'**Alec Allen**'–1982 (Carpenter). Evergreen. 26 in. Early midseason. 5½ in., round, ruffled, creamy yellow self, with lime-green throat. Diploid.

'**Antarctica**'–1980 (Peck). Dormant. 27 in. Midseason. Large 6 in., light cream self with green throat. Tetraploid.

'**Atlanta Supreme**'–1984 (Petree). Semi-evergreen. 30 in. Midseason. Superb, lightly ruffled, and textured 6 in., light yellow self, with green throat. Tetraploid.

'Atlanta Supreme'. Photo by PETREE

'**Barcelona Belle**'–1983 (Elizabeth Hudson Salter). Evergreen. 16 in. Early midseason. Round, full, overlapped 2½ in., palest lemon-cream, with bright chartreuse heart. Diploid.

'**Baseball**'–1974 (Durio). Evergreen. 26 in. Early midseason. A medium large, 5 in., round, full formed, tailored, ivory-cream with green throat. Diploid.

'**Biarritz**'–1982 (Munson). Evergreen. 26 in. Midseason. Large, 6 in., full overlapping form, cream-yellow with delicate shadings of yellow, flesh and pink. Yellow-green throat. Diploid.

'**Brocaded Gown**'–1979 (Millikan). Semi-evergreen. 28 in. Early midseason. Large, bold, ruffled, 6 in., lemon-cream self, with chartreuse throat. Very special. Diploid.

'**Burmese Sunlight**'–1984 (Munson). Evergreen. 18 in. Early midseason. Large, 6 in., full-formed, round, ruffled, cream-yellow and pink, edged in strong yellow. Large cream-chartreuse throat. Tetraploid.

'**Butter Pat**'–1970 (Kennedy). Dormant. 20 in. Midseason. Very fine miniature, light yellow self, that is nicely ruffled and clumps fast. A classic. Diploid.

'Brocaded Gown'. Photo by MILLIKAN

'**Cabbage Flower**'–1984 (Kirchhoff). Evergreen. 20 in. Early midseason. Medium large, double, cream lemon-yellow. Chartreuse throat. Special. Diploid.

'**Cafe Society**'–1982 (Pierce). Semievergreen. 18 in. Midseason. Large, triangular, 6 in., ruffled, cream-yellow self, with green throat. Diploid.

'Cafe Society'. Photo by PIERCE

'**Chardonnay**'–1984 (Kirchhoff). Semievergreen. 20 in. Early. A medium, 4½ in., double, cream-white, with yellow halo and chartreuse throat. Diploid.

'**Charlie Baker**'–1985 (Gates). Evergreen. 26 in. Early. Elegant, large, 6½ in., cream-yellow self with green throat. Broad, full, ruffled, handsome form.

'**Chateau Chardonnay**'–1986 (Moldovan). Dormant. 30 in. Early midseason. Superb, large, flat 7½ in., cream to ivory-yellow and pink-yellow blend with green throat. Tetraploid.

'**Cotton Club**'–1985 (Kirchhoff). Evergreen. 20 in. Early midseason. Superb, 5 in., double, butter-cream self, with green throat and an elegant double form. Diploid.

'Chardonnay'. Photo by KIRCHHOFF

'Chateau Chardonnay'. Photo by MOLDOVAN

'Cotton Club'. Photo by KIRCHHOFF

'Crystal Charm'–1982 (Elizabeth Hudson Salter). Evergreen. 16 in. Early midseason. Full, round, flat, and ruffled, 2½ in., pale cream-ivory, with an intense lime heart and raised pink midribs. Very heavy substance. Diploid.

'Czars Champagne'–1980 (Munson). Evergreen. 24 in. Midseason. Broad, full, ruffled, medium 5 in., cream-ivory and champagne with ivory-yellow-green throat. Tetraploid.

'Dalai Lama'–1975 (Moldovan). Dormant. 24 in. Midseason late. Medium 5½ in., wide, full, cream-yellow edged gold, with green throat. A classic. Tetraploid.

'Edna Spalding Memorial'–1968 (MacMillan). Dormant. 16 in. Early midseason. Large, broad, full, ruffled, lemon-yellow-green, with green throat. A treasure. Diploid.

'Either Way'–1985 (Durio). Evergreen. 34 in. Early midseason. 6 in., exciting, double lemon-yellow-cream, with ruffled petals and sepals that are crepelike, ribbed, and diamond dusted. Has both single and double blooms. Tetraploid.

'Ellen Christine'–1987 (Crochet). Evergreen. 24 in. Midseason. An interesting blend of cream-yellow and pink makes this large, 6 in., ruffled and textured, double with green-gold throat, superb. Diploid.

'Ellen Christine'. Photo by CROCHET

'Elves Lemonade'–1981 (Elizabeth Hudson Salter). Evergreen. 20 in. Midseason to late. A small, 3 in., pale lemon ice with tiny green heart and pale cream-white midribs. Diploid.

'Eskimo'–1971 (Durio). Evergreen. 26 in. Midseason. A large, broad, full, and ruffled, cream-yellow self, with white midribs, and strong green throat. Tetraploid.

'Evening Bell'–1971 (Peck). Dormant. 26 in. Midseason. Large, 7 in., creped, and ruffled, lemon-yellow self with chartreuse throat. Tetraploid.

'Fred Ham'–1982 (Munson). Evergreen. 24 in. Early midseason. Large, voluptuous, 7 in., flat, ruffled, fluted, gold edged lemon-cream, with lemon-chartreuse throat. Very special. Tetraploid.

'Garden Goddess'–1974 (Munson). Semievergreen. 28 in. Early midseason. Large, 5 in., ivory-cream yellow, with heavy, waxlike substance, and a small yellow-green heart. Tetraploid.

'Gaza'–1982 (Durio). Evergreen. 26 in. Early midseason. Large, handsome, 6 in., creped cream-yellow, with broad segments, and heavy substance. Tetraploid.

'Great Connections'–1983 (Peck). Dormant. 21 in. Midseason. Beautiful, 6 in., light cream self with green-yellow throat and distinctive, full, ruffled, form. Tetraploid.

'Green Dolphin Street'–1986 (Sanford Roberts). Evergreen. 28 in. Early midseason. 7½ in., tailored, greenish yellow spider, with chartreuse throat. Tetraploid.

'Green Puff'–1977 (W. Spalding). Semievergreen. 20 in. Midseason. Medium large, round, full formed, yellow-chartreuse, with a green throat. Very Fine. Diploid.

'Hoopskirt'–1986 (Millikan). Dormant. 21 in. Midseason. Medium sized, 5 in., cream-lemon-yellow blend with light green deep in throat. Form is broad and overlapped. Diploid.

'Hoopskirt'. Photo by MILLIKAN

'Ida Duke Miles'–1984 (Webster). Dormant. 18 in. Midseason. Very ruffled, 6 in., light yellow self, with small green throat. Tetraploid.

'Inez Ways'–1975 (Durio). Evergreen. 20 in. Early. 7½ in., very large, cream-yellow self, with creped, very wide, ruffled, overlapped segments, yellow-green throat. Tetraploid.

'Irresistible Impulse'–1986 (Stamile). Dormant. 30 in. Midseason late. 5 in., ruffled, deep lemon-yellow self, with green throat. Diploid.

'Jade Lady'–1984 (Munson). Evergreen. 24 in. Early midseason. Large, 6 in., round, overlapped, cream-yellow, chartreuse, chrome and lemon blend, the throat is deep chrome-chartreuse that radiates throughout the flower thus giving a greenish glow. Tetraploid.

'Irresistible Impulse'. Photo by STAMILE

'Kallista'–1985 (Munson). Semievergreen. 20 in. Early to late. Ruffled and overlapped, large, 6 in., pastel cream-yellow with waxlike substance. Pale green throat. Tetraploid.

'Kecia'–1977 (Munson). Semievergreen. 28 in. Early midseason. 6 in., large, ruffled, flat cream-yellow blend with a green throat. A classic. Tetraploid.

'Kewanee'–1986 (Oscie B. Whatley). Semievergreen. 28 in. Midseason to late. Round, broad, ruffled, 5 in., cream-yellow, with green throat and white midribs. Diploid.

'Kewanee'. Photo by WHATLEY

'Lemon Jade'–1983 (Munson). Evergreen. 24 in. Early midseason to midseason. Round, recurved, lightly creped textured, 5 in., superb, lemon and pink blend, with a strong lemon-lime throat. The entire flower is washed lightly in chartreuse giving a special glow. Extra special. Tetraploid.

'Ludie'–1983 (Webster). Dormant. 18 in. Midseason. Beautiful, ruffled, large, 6 in., ivory-cream yellow, with very small, green throat. Very well branched. Tetraploid.

'Lunar Sea'–1982 (Munson). Evergreen. 22 in. Early midseason. Elegant, 6 in., large, full, round, very ruffled, and frilled lemon-cream with chartreuse throat. Tetraploid.

46

'Ludie'. Photo by WEBSTER

'Nan Durio'. Photo by DURIO

'Marble Faum'–1983 (Millikan). Evergreen. 20 in. Early. Incredibly formed, 5 in., cream marbled with lemon-yellow and light green throat. Round, ruffled, fluted, and flat. A milestone in breeding. Diploid.

'Marble Faun'. Photo by MILLIKAN

'Nan Durio'–1986 (Durio). Evergreen. 28 in. Early midseason. Very large, recurved, 7 in., ruffled, and fluted, light creamy yellow touched with flesh-pink, with an olive-green throat. Elegant and unique. Tetraploid.

'Osaka'–1986 (Durio). Evergreen. 24 in. Early midseason. A large to very large, handsome cream-yellow of full round form, with lightly creped texture. Midribs are a pale flesh-pink, and throat is green-chartreuse. Very fine, special, and incredibly beautiful. Tetraploid.

'Pasta'–1978 (Durio). Evergreen. 30 in. Early midseason. 7 in., large and imposing, beautifully formed, cream-yellow of creped texture, with lime-green throat. Petals and sepals are ruffled, ribbed, fluted, and recurved. Impressive. Diploid.

'Pasta'. Photo by DURIO

'Robert Way Schlumpf'–1967 (MacMillan). Evergreen. 36 in. Early midseason. Tall, ivory to cream-white, a classic, with full form, fluted petals and a small, green throat. Diploid.

'Ruffled Double Frills'–1986 (E. C. Brown). Semievergreen. 24 in. Early midseason. 5 in., double, greenish yellow self, with green throat. Diploid.

'Ruffled Double Frills'. Photo by BROWN, E.C.

'Ruffled Masterpiece'–1987 (E. C. Brown). Semievergreen. 26 in. Midseason. Large, voluptuous, 6 in., cream to light yellow pink-buff, that is very very ruffled, with green-yellow throat, and lighter midribs. Diploid.

'Ruffled Masterpiece'. Photo by BROWN, E.C.

'Sea Goddess'–1984 (Munson). Evergreen. 26 in. Early midseason. Broad, recurved, large, 6 in., creamy lemon-chartreuse, with a large, green throat, that blends into the petal color, giving a greenish glint to the flowers. A creamy midrib adds to the total picture. Tetraploid.

'Spanish Lemon'–1983 (Munson). Evergreen. 26 in. Midseason to late. 6 in., large, flat, broadly formed, pale lemon-cream and chartreuse, brushed with delicate pink highlights. Tetraploid.

'Spring Willow Song'–1983 (Munson). Semievergreen. 26 in. Early midseason. Round, ruffled, broad, and opulent, 6 in., lemon-yellow that is incredulity flat, waxy, and of heavy substance, with small, green throat. Tetraploid.

'Sugar Cookie'–1983 (Apps). Evergreen. 21 in. Early midseason. 3½ in., small-flowered cream self with green throat. Diploid.

'Sugar Cookie'. Photo by APPS

'Tom Collins'–1982 (Millikan). Dormant. 26 in. Early midseason. Round, crisp, voluptuous, 4 in., green-yellow self, with green throat. Diploid.

'Tom Collins'. Photo by MILLIKAN

'Top Honors'–1976 (Childs). Semievergreen. 24 in. Early midseason. 7½ in., very large, wide petaled, lemon-cream self with green throat, that is stunning in beauty and performance. A classic, and very fine. Diploid.

'Yard Master'–1981 (Oscie B. Whatley). Dormant. 28 in. Midseason. A fine, textured, and lightly ruffled, large, 6½ in., medium cream-yellow, with green throat, and white midribs. Tetraploid.

'Yard Master'. Photo by WHATLEY

'Zenar'–1986 (Oscie B. Whatley). Semievergreen. 20 in. Early midseason. Superb, round, full, broad, lightly ruffled, light yellow self, with green throat. Diploid.

'Atlanta Fringe Benefit'–1985 (Petree). Dormant. 21 in. Early midseason. Very ruffled, and creped, 5 in., medium yellow self, with green throat. Tetraploid.

'Atlanta Full House'–1984 (Petree). Dormant. 27 in. Midseason. 6½ in., yellow self, with green throat. Tetraploid.

'Avon Many Moons'–1982 (Moldovan). Dormant. 26 in. Early midseason. Large, broad, full and round lemon-yellow, with chartreuse throat. Tetraploid.

'Betty Woods'–1980 (Kirchhoff). Evergreen. 26 in. Early midseason. A sensational, ruffled, broad petaled, 5½ in., double, Chinese-yellow, with a green heart. Presently the definitive yellow double. Diploid.

'Betty Woods'. Photo by KIRCHHOFF

'Bombay Lemon'–1982 (Munson). Evergreen. 22 in. Early midseason. Bold, handsome, 6 in., large flowers of ivory-lemon, with a chartreuse heart. Diploid.

'Bonnie John Seton'–1967 (Peck). Dormant. 26 in. Early midseason. 7 in., yellow self, with green throat. Tetraploid.

'Brendan'–1987 (Durio). Evergreen. 28 in. Early midseason. Large, recurved, 7 in. flower, with pie crust edge, colored in a bright canary-yellow self, with a strong olive-green throat. Tetraploid.

'Brilliant Luster'–1982 (W. Spalding). Evergreen. 17 in. Early. Large, ruffled, 6½ in., yellow, with pink midribs and yellow-green throat. Diploid.

'Butter Yellow'–1974 (Monette). Evergreen. 26 in. Early midseason. The bold, 8 in., large, flowers are broad, flat and spectacular. Color is butter-yellow. Diploid.

'Capella Light'–1980 (Munson). Evergreen. 28 in. Early midseason. A 6 in., large, yellow self, with chartreuse throat. Tetraploid.

'Brendan'. Photo by DURIO

'Carondelet'–1973 (Oscie B. Whatley). Dormant. 21 in. Midseason. Round, umbrella-shaped, 5 in., light green-yellow self, with green throat. A milestone in breeding. Diploid.

'Cleda Jones'–1985 (Chesnick). Dormant. 30 in. Early midseason. 6 in., yellow-gold self. Pale green throat. Elegant. Tetraploid.

'Clifford Warren'–1986 (W. Spalding). Dormant. 18 in. Midseason. Large, round, ruffled, chartreuse-yellow self, with very green throat. Diploid.

'Crystal Cupid'–1985 (Elizabeth Hudson Salter). Evergreen. 14 in. Early midseason. A very round, full, and overlapped, 2¼ in., bright lemon-yellow, with a deeply etched and ruffled edge. Diploid.

'Darrell'–1981 (Durio). Evergreen. 26 in. Early midseason. Large, 7 in., light butter-yellow, lightly touched flesh, with chartreuse throat. Broad, ruffled, showy form. Special, with incredible vigor. Tetraploid.

'Double Barrell'–1982 (Durio). Semievergreen. 24 in. Early midseason. Large, 6½ in., double, full, ruffled, symmetrical bright light yellow self, with lime-green throat. Tetraploid.

'Ed Kirchhoff'–1981 (David Kirchhoff). Semievergreen. 26 in. Midseason. Large, very ruffled, medium yellow self, of wide, full, form, with olive-green throat. Tetraploid.

'Ever So Ruffled'–1983 (Stamile). Evergreen. 22 in. Midseason. Round, very special, 5 in., very ruffled, very broad petaled, deep yellow, lighter midribs, green throat. Tetraploid.

'Ever So Ruffled'. Photo by STAMILE

'Estelle Whitmire'–1976 (E. W. Brown). Evergreen. 28 in. Early midseason. A very large, tailored 7, ¼ in., broad petaled, chartreuse-yellow, with lemon-lime throat. Diploid.

'Floyd Cove'–1987 (Stamile). Dormant. 21 in., Midseason. 5 in. round, recurved, and boldly ruffled, butter-yellow, with green throat. Tetraploid.

'Floyd Cove'. Photo by STAMILE

'Fortune's Choice'–1981 (Elizabeth Hudson Salter). Semievergreen. 15 in. Early midseason. 2¾ in., slightly triangular, heavily ruffled, and frilled, clear lemon-cream-yellow, with a deep green heart. Well branched scapes, with multiple blooms. A truly beautiful garden flower. Diploid.

'Jeweled Sunbeam'–1985 (Elizabeth Hudson Salter). Evergreen. 15 in. A tiny, 2 in., delicately formed flower, of the most pristine yellow. Flowers are very round, full, overlapped, and finely ruffled. A jewel of a flower. Diploid.

'Joel'–1978 (Harris). Dormant. 24 in. Early midseason. Elegant and special, 5½ in., yellow self, with green throat. Tetraploid.

'Fortune's Choice'. Photo by SALTER

'Limon'–1975 (Yancey). Semievergreen. 13 in. Early. Small, 4 in., lemon-yellow self, with green throat. Diploid.

'Limon'. Photo by MALLORY

'Lion Dance'–1986 (Harris-Benz). Dormant. 26 in. Midseason. Large, showy, 6 in., very ruffled, heavy textured, butter-yellow, with lighter midribs, and green throat. Tetraploid.

'Lion Dance'. Photo by MERCER

'Most Noble'–1980 (Munson). Evergreen. 26 in. Early midseason. Large, handsome, broad, full, round and ruffled, strong lemon self, with green throat. Very elegant. Tetraploid.

'My Ways'–1975 (Wild). Dormant. 25 in. Early midseason. Large, 6 in., yellow self, with green throat. A standard and a classic. Diploid.

'Olive Alice Pauley'–1983 (Munson). Semievergreen. 30 in. Midseason. Elegant and special, large, 6 in., lemon-cream-yellow, with broadly, overlapped, heavily ruffled segments, chartreuse throat. Tetraploid.

'Quiet Beauty'–1985 (Stamile). Dormant. 28 in. Early midseason. A medium-large, 5½ in., corduroy textured, broadly formed, and lightly ruffled, butter-yellow self, with green throat. Diploid.

'Quiet Beauty'. Photo by STAMILE

'Sabie'–1974 (MacMillan). Evergreen. 24 in. Early midseason. A great classic, medium yellow, very broad, full, ruffled form, and a green throat. A major breeder for voluptuous formed, yellows and pastels. Diploid.

'Sanctus Bell'–1980 (Moldovan). Dormant. 30 in. Midseason. Large, round, ruffled, showy, lemon-yellow self. Tetraploid.

'Siloam Bill Ater'–1984 (R. Henry). Dormant. 20 in., Midseason. Elegant, round and flat, 6 in., with very ruffled petals. Color is clear yellow self, with green throat. Diploid.

'Siloam Bill Ater'. Photo by HENRY

'Siloam Full Circle'–1983 (R. Henry). Dormant. 22 in. Midseason late. 5 in., yellow self, with green throat. Diploid.

'Siloam Irish Prize'–1987 (R. Henry). Dormant. 20 in., Midseason. Recurved and ruffled, 5 in., yellow self, with green throat. Diploid.

'Siloam Irish Prize'. Photo by HENRY

'Siloam Mama'–1982 (R. Henry). Dormant. 24 in. Early midseason. 5¾ in., yellow self, with green throat. Diploid.

'Spanish Jade'–1978 (Munson). Evergreen. 28 in. Early midseason. Medium-large, 5 in., flowers are wide, full, and broad petaled, blend of yellow, flesh and cream-pink. The lime color of the throat radiates out into the petal color, giving the flower a greenish glow. Tetraploid.

'Springtime Sonata'–1975 (W. Spalding). Semievergreen. 21 in. Early midseason. A large, 6 in., ruffled, pastel yellow self, with green throat. Elegant and distinctive. Diploid.

'Sunbow'. Photo by ALLGOOD

'Sunbow'–1978 (Yancey). Semievergreen. 24 in. Early midseason. 5 in., round, flat, ruffled, bright yellow self, with green throat. Bold handsome form. A show stopper. Diploid.

'Sun King'–1980 (Munson). Evergreen.

30 in. Early midseason. 6 in., large, yellow, with shadings of gold and cream, round, overlapped segments, deeply ruffled, and fluted. Yellow-green throat. Special. Tetraploid.

'Suns Eye'–1978 (Ed Kirchhoff). Semi-evergreen. 32 in. Early midseason. Medium, large, 5 in., bright yellow self, of creped texture, broad, full, voluptuous form, and small, green throat. Tetraploid.

'Sunshine Prize'–1978 (E. W. Brown).

Evergreen. 22 in. Early. 6¼ in., voluptuous, golden yellow self, with yellow-green throat. Bold and showy. Tetraploid.

'Yellow Kitten'–1979 (W. Spalding). Evergreen. 17 in. Early midseason. 4½ in., medium, pale yellow self, with green throat. Form is round, flat, and full. Diploid.

'Wynnson'–1977 (Criswell). Dormant. 24 in. Early midseason. 4½ in., broad, ruffled and fluted, cream-yellow self with small, green heart. Diploid.

GOLD THROUGH ORANGE

'Anna'–1982 (Harris). Dormant. 22 in. Midseason. 4½ in., medium, wide, ruffled, golden orange self, with gold-green throat. Tetraploid.

'Autumn Countess'–1983 (Elizabeth Hudson Salter). Evergreen. 15 in. Midseason. Very full formed, ruffled, triangular, 2¾ in., bright orange, with a hint of pink underlay. A tiny, olive heart. Grasslike foliage. Diploid.

'By Myself'–1971 (Peck). Dormant. 30 in. Midseason. Large, broad, full, ruffled, light gold self. It is a daylily classic. Tetraploid.

'Camden Gold Dollar'–1982 (Yancey). Evergreen. 22 in. Early midseason. A miniature, very full and wide, ruffled, and a bright golden yellow. A special small one. Diploid.

'Cavaliers Gold'–1979 (Elizabeth Hudson Salter). Evergreen. 13 in. Early midseason. 2¼ in., deep gold self, of round, full,

overlapped form, with slightly creped petals and sepals that recurve, and a small, olive-green heart. Diploid.

'Cornwall'–1966 (Lambert). Dormant. 30 in. Early midseason. Large, 6 in., flat, roundish, ruffled, deep orange-gold self. Diploid.

'Creole Heir'–1984 (Guidry). Semievergreen. 24 in. Midseason. 4¼ in., gold with a pink blush, and green throat. Diploid.

'Demetrius'–1977 (Harris). Dormant. 24 in. Early midseason. 5½ in., medium-large, ruffled, orange-gold-yellow self, with green throat. Tetraploid.

'Earth Angel'–1987 (Stamile). Dormant. 25 in. Early midseason. Wonderful, 4½ in., medium, very ruffled, broad petaled, apricot-gold self, with green throat. Tetraploid.

'Creole Heir'. Photo by GUIDRY

'Earth Angel'. Photo by STAMILE

'Glory Days'–1987 (Stamile). Dormant. 24 in. Midseason late. 5½ in., flat, voluptuous, broad petaled, ruffled, gold self, with green-gold throat. Very special and very beautiful. Tetraploid.

'Glory Days'. Photo by STAMILE

'Golden Pond'–1982 (Peck). Dormant. 25 in. Midseason. Large, 6 in., flower, with a deep, pie crust, ruffled, edge. Color is a light gold self, with yellow-green throat. Tetraploid.

'Golden Prize'–1968 (Peck). Dormant. 26 in. Late. Large, flat, 7 in., gold self. A classic. Tetraploid.

'Goldie Hicks'–1982 (Durio). Evergreen. 30 in. Early midseason. Handsome, 7 in., very large, broad-petaled, roundish, tailored, gold self, with green-gold throat. Special. Tetraploid.

'Houston'–1980 (Durio). Evergreen. 28 in. Early midseason. A large, 6 in., showy, creped yellow-gold self, of round, full, recurved form, with a green-gold throat. Tetraploid.

'Imperial Condor'–1986 (Moldovan). Dormant. 35 in. Midseason. Very large, 8 in., pie crust edged, gold self, with green throat. Handsome and spectacular. Tetraploid.

'Imperial Condor'. Photo by MOLDOVAN

'Jamie Douglas'–1967 (Peck). Dormant. 26 in. Late. 7 in., large, deep gold self. Tetraploid.

'Joyful Sentinel'–1984 (Elizabeth Hudson Salter). Semievergreen. 18 in. Early midseason. Very full, round, overlapped, 2¾ in., bright, intense, gold self, with tiny, olive heart. Diploid.

'Little Sun Singer'–1986 (Elizabeth Hudson Salter). Semievergreen. 14 in. Early midseason. A very bright, round, fully formed, 2 in., pure yellow-gold. A sunny addition to any garden. Diploid.

'Moroccan Summer'–1986 (Kirchhoff). Evergreen. 22 in. Early midseason. Special, 4¾ in., double, of intense, gold self, with green throat. Diploid.

'Moroccan Summer'. Photo by KIRCHOFF

'Munchkin Moon'–1975 (Elizabeth Hudson Salter). Evergreen. 16 in. Early midseason. 2¾ in., lightly ruffled, gold-yellow and gold-apricot blend, with green throat. A classic miniature. Diploid.

'Pearl Lewis'–1984 (Peck). Dormant. 26 in. Midseason late. Large, 6 in., broad, voluptuous, slightly recurved, ruffled, gold self, with green-gold throat. Tetraploid.

'Pearl Lewis'. Photo by PECK

'Petite Prince'–1983 (Elizabeth Hudson Salter). Evergreen. 14 in. Early midseason. A tiny, 1¾ in., apricot, pink and gold blend, with a deeper apricot veining, that carries from the orange throat. A deep set, olive heart. Diploid.

'Rachel My Love'–1983 (Talbott). Evergreen. 18 in. Early midseason. Large, well formed, voluptuous, double, of a clear golden yellow. Special. Diploid.

'Saffron Glow'–1980 (Peck). Dormant. 27 in. Midseason. Medium large, elegantly ruffled, light gold-yellow self, with green-gold throat, with wide, ruffled, petals. Tetraploid.

'Sheer Class'–1983 (Peck). Dormant. 26 in. Midseason. Large, 6 in., ruffled, light gold self, with olive throat. Form is strongly reflexed. Tetraploid.

'Siloam Andrew Trotter'. Photo by HENRY

'Spanish Serenade'. Photo by GUIDRY

'Sheer Class'. Photo by PECK

'Shockwave'–1978 (E. W. Brown). Semievergreen. 30 in. Early midseason. Large, 6 in., broad petaled, fully formed, yellow-gold self, with gold throat. Boldly handsome. Tetraploid.

'Siloam Andrew Trotter'–1983 (R. Henry). Dormant. 26 in. Late. Medium-large, 5 in., heavily ruffled, elegant, gold self, with green throat. Grand! Diploid.

'Siloam Gold Coin'–1981 (R. Henry). Dormant. 18 in. Midseason. Round, 4¼ in., gold self, with small green throat. Special. Diploid.

'Spanish Serenade'–1987 (Guidry). Evergreen. 26 in. Midseason. Elegant, 5 in., well formed, frilled, apricot, with green throat. Diploid.

'Sparkling Orange'–1983 (Barth). Dormant. 34 in., Early midseason. Very fine, 6 in., large, brilliant gold-orange self. Tetraploid.

'Tiffany Gold'–1982 (Munson). Ever-green. 24 in. Early midseason. Very large, creped and ruffled, gold-yellow self, with broad, full, overlapping segments. Gold throat. Spectacular! Diploid.

'Yazoo Banana Peel'–1984 (W. H. Smith). Semievergreen. 30 in. Early midseason. An interesting, 10 in., pale gold, spider, with cream throat. Diploid.

'Yazoo Banana Peel'. Photo by SMITH

'Yellow Fever'–1972 (W. Spalding). Semievergreen. 20 in. Early midseason. 6 in., medium-large, ruffled and recurved, yellow-gold self, of waxy texture, with a green throat. A classic. Diploid.

'Willis And Hattie'–1982 (R. Henry). Dormant. 20 in. Midseason late. Large, 6½ in., gold self, with green throat. Diploid.

'Abex'–1983 (Whatley). Dormant. 20 in. Midseason. A medium-large, dark red self, with a yellow-green throat. Elegantly formed and handsomely ruffled. Sun resistant. Tetraploid.

'Acapulco Flame'–1986 (Sanford Roberts). Semievergreen. 28 in. Early midseason. 5 in., bright, ruffled, red self, with green-yellow throat. Tetraploid.

'Acapulco Flame'. Photo by ROBERTS

'Acapulco Sunset'–1983 (Sanford Roberts). Semievergreen. 22 in. Early midseason. A medium, 4½–5 in. red self, broad, full, elegant and smoothly tailored. Sun resistant. Tetraploid.

'Amadeus'–1981 (Kirchhoff). Semievergreen. 26 in. Early midseason. A boldly formed, 5½ in., scarlet self, with yellow-green throat. Sun resistant. Tetraploid.

'Angel Fire'–1986 (Varner). Dormant. 30 in. Midseason. 5 in., scarlet-ruby-red self, with very, green throat. Tetraploid.

'Angel Fire'. Photo by VARNER

'Angus McLeod'–1985 (Mercer). Dormant. 26 in. Midseason late. Handsome, rich dark red self, with yellow-green throat. A consummate grower. Tetraploid.

'Angus McLeod'. Photo by MERCER

'Avante Garde'–1986 (Moldovan). Dormant. 26 in. Early midseason. A bold, uniquely colored, 5½ in., flower of orange-red, with amber and tan borders, with yellow-green throat. Tetraploid.

'Avante Garde'. Photo by MOLDOVAN

'Aztec Furnace'–1986 (Stamile). Dormant. 27 in. Early midseason. A russet-red, with deeper red eye zone and green throat. Elegantly formed. Tetraploid.

'Bama Bound'–1986 (Webster). Dormant. 28 in. Midseason. 5¼ in., very bright, dark red self, with small, green throat. Tetraploid.

'Beasley'–1979 (Peck). Dormant. 26 in. Midseason. 6½ in., large, wide, fully formed, deep red, with small yellow-green throat. A classic red. Tetraploid.

'Big Apple'–1986 (Sellers). Semievergreen. 26 in. Early midseason. A handsome, 5 in., flower of rich cerise-red, and a bold, green throat. Unique. Diploid.

'Aztec Furnace'. Photo by STAMILE

'Bama Bound'. Photo by WEBSTER

'Big Apple'. Photo by MERCER

'Billye Red'–1983 (Dove). Semievergreen. 24 in. Early midseason. Broad, full, and ruffled lightly, 5 in., red self, with light lime-green throat. Diploid.

'Blood Spot'–1983 (Millikan). Semievergreen. 25 in. Midseason late. Broad, full, tailored, special, 4½ in., blood-red self, with slightly darker eye zone, and a small, lime-green throat. Tetraploid.

'Bobby Red'–1982 (Dove). Semievergreen. 18 in. Early midseason. Broad, ruffled, 5½ in., bright red self, with lime-green throat. Diploid.

'Bologongo'–1986 (Weston). Dormant. 16 in. Midseason. Broad, flat, tailored, 5½ in., Chinese-red self, with a yellow-green throat. Diploid.

'Bologongo'. Photo by WESTON

'Carolyn Hendrix'–1987 (Munson). Semievergreen. 26 in. Midseason. Broad, ruffled, fully formed, 5 in., rose-red self, with yellow-green throat. Tetraploid.

'Carolyn Hendrix'. Photo by MUNSON

'Chicago Apache'–1981 (Marsh-Klehm). Dormant. 27 in. Midseason. 5 in., medium-large, broad petaled, ruffled, scarlet-red self, with yellow-green throat. Tetraploid.

'Chicago Ruby'–1977 (Marsh). Semievergreen. 30 in. Midseason. 6 in., large, broad, full, ruby-red, with small, green throat. Tetraploid.

'Chinatown'–1980 (Munson). Dormant. 22 in. Midseason. Medium, 5 in., bright, and intense, velvety, orangey red, with a small, lemon throat, and a heart of green. Tetraploid.

'Christmas Is'–1979 (Yancey). Dormant. 26 in. Early midseason. 4½ in., medium, deep red, with a large, bold, sunburst throat, of lime-chartreuse. A classic. Diploid.

'Christmas Is'. Photo by ALLGOOD

'Christmas Story'–1985 (Stamile). Semi-evergreen. 29 in. Midseason. A large, ruffled, beautifully formed, 5½ in., cerise-red. Diploid.

'Christmas Story'. Photo by STAMILE

'Cranberry Cove'–1985 (Stamile). Dormant. 28 in. Early midseason. A full form, wide petaled, lightly ruffled, 4¼ in., cranberry-red self, small, green throat. Diploid.

'Cranberry Cove'. Photo by STAMILE

'Dawn Piper'–1987 (Elliott). Semievergreen. 20 in. Midseason. Medium, voluptuous, rose-red self, with deep red eye zone, and yellow-green throat. Diploid.

'Double Trouble'–1986 (Webster). Dormant. 24 in. Midseason. 4½ in., dark red double, with yellow-green throat. Tetraploid.

'Double Trouble'. Photo by WEBSTER

'Douglas Dale'–1968 (Peck). Dormant. 24 in., Midseason. 6 in. red blend, with green throat. Tetraploid.

'Douglas Potter'–1982 (Mayfield). Semievergreen. 25 in. Early midseason. Broad, full, 4½ in., blood-red self, with green throat. Excellent sun resistance. Diploid.

'Eleventh Hour'–1977 (Peck). Dormant. 25 in. Midseason. Handsome, 6½ in., medium-large, rich, velvety, dark blackish red self, with green throat. Tetraploid.

'Fire Arrow'–1985 (Webster). Dormant. 24 in. Midseason. 8½ in., bright red spider, with chartreuse throat. Tetraploid.

'Fire Arrow'. Photo by WEBSTER

'Firepower'–1984 (E. W. Brown). Evergreen. 25 in. Early midseason. Large, tailored, 6 in., flower of barn-red, with gold-green throat. Incredible vigor. Tetraploid.

'Gato'–1981 (Durio). Dormant. 28 in. Midseason. Medium-large, wide petaled, rich dark red, with small, circular yellow throat, with a green heart. Extremely fine. Tetraploid.

'Gato'. Photo by DURIO

'Gene Foster'–1984 (Munson). Dormant. 24 in. Early midseason. 6 in., large, broadly formed, roundish, intense rose-cherry-red self, with a velvet sheen. A round, circular, yellow-gold throat, gold-green heart. Tetraploid.

'Gene Foster'. Photo by MUNSON

'Gentle Dragon'–1975 (Peck). Dormant. 29 in. Early midseason. 6½in., rich, bright cherry-red self, with green throat. Tetraploid.

'Grand Opera'–1978 (Munson). Semi-evergreen. 28 in. Midseason. 6 in., large, brilliant cherry to rose-red, flat, ruffled, and fluted. Small, yellow-green throat. Tetraploid.

'Hermitage Copernicus'–1985 (Lambert). Dormant. 28 in. Midseason. Superbly formed, large, 6 in., large, crimson-red self, with yellow-green throat. Tetraploid.

'Hermitage Darwin'–1985 (Lambert). Dormant. 32 in. Early midseason. Handsome, large, very ruffled, 6 in., rose-red self, with apricot throat. Tetraploid.

'Hermitage Darwin'. Photo by LAMBERT

'Hermitage Newton'–1983 (Lambert). Dormant. 30 in. Midseason. Large, 6 in., mahogany, edge in gold, with a unique, patterned yellow-green throat. Tetraploid.

'Highland Lord'–1983 (Munson). Dormant. 22 in. Midseason late. A large, round, overlapped, ruffled, deep rich velvety, red, double. Petaloids are bordered, with an ivory-gold, wirelike edge. Tetraploid.

'Illini Blessing'–1984 (Varner). Dormant. 31 in. Midseason. Medium, 5 in., medium, ruffled, dark red, with darker veins, and medium green throat. Tetraploid.

'Illini Fire'–1981 (Varner). Dormant. 36 in. Midseason. Very fine, 4½ in., double red self, with light green throat. Tetraploid.

'Illini Maiden'–1981 (Varner). Dormant. 36 in. Midseason. 5 in., very dark red, with wirelike, white edge, and green throat. Tetraploid.

'Illini Maiden'. Photo by VARNER

'**Illini Model**'–1984 (Varner). Dormant. 36 in. Early midseason. 5 1/2 in., dark red self, with green throat. Tetraploid.

'**Illini Show Girl**'–1984 (Varner). Dormant. 32 in. Midseason. Super, 6 in., deep dark red self, with a very green throat. Tetraploid.

'Illini Show Girl'. Photo by VARNER

'**James Marsh**'–1978 (Marsh-Klehm). Dormant. 26 in. Early midseason. Medium-large, bright, velvety, scarlet-red, with ruffled petals. Throat is small and yellow-green. Tetraploid.

'**Jessie James**'–1984 (Peck). Dormant. 22 in. Midseason. Special, 5 in., bright scarlet, of broad, overlapped, form and small, green-yellow throat. Tetraploid.

'Jessie James'. Photo by MERCER

'**Jim Watson**'–1982 (E. C. Brown). Evergreen. 26 in. Early midseason. Handsomely formed, 5 in., red self, with lime-green throat. Diploid.

'**Jog On**'–1978 (Peck). Dormant. 30 in. Midseason. Bold, 5½ in., scarlet self, with yellow-green throat. Frequently is double. Tetraploid.

'**Kacie Boy**'–1983 (Durio). Evergreen. 25 in. Early. Attractive, broadly formed, 4 in., ruby-red self, with green-chartreuse throat. Diploid.

'**Lilliputian Knight**'–1974 (Elizabeth Hudson Salter). Semievergreen. 16 in. Midseason to late. 2½ in., very round, fully formed, bright, deep rose-red, with bright green heart. Diploid.

'**Little Red Warbler**'–1985 (Crochet). Dormant. 18 in. Early midseason. 3 in., recurved, dark red, with a deep maroon eye zone, and yellow-green throat. All segments recurve. On an established plant, has super bud count. Diploid.

'Little Red Warbler'. Photo by CROCHET

'**Lonnie**'–1969 (Lambert). Dormant. 30 in. Midseason. Unique, 7 in., bright red self, with green throat. Diploid.

'**Lord Camden**'–1974 (Kennedy). Dormant. 24 in. Midseason. Special, 4¼ in., bright crimson-raspberry self, with a green throat. Diploid.

'**Lukey Boy**'–1983 (Durio). Dormant. 26 in. Early midseason. Fine, broad petaled 4 in. bright red self with chartreuse-green throat. Diploid.

'**Madame Curie**'–1986 (Moldovan). Dormant. 28 in. Early midseason. Unique, 6 in., cerise-red and rose-pink blend, with yellow-green throat. Tetraploid.

'Madame Curie'. Photo by MOLDOVAN

'Merle Kent'–1980 (Munson). Evergreen. 28 in. Midseason. Special, 6 in., large, broad petaled, bright orange-red, with green throat. Tetraploid.

'Misha'–1982 (Peck). Dormant. 26 in. Midseason. Elegantly formed, 4 in., bright orange-red self, with green throat. Tetraploid.

'Monte Carlo Red'–1986 (Munson). Semievergreen. 32 in. Midseason. Broad, voluptuous, overlapped, 6 in., medium rose-red, tinted, and highlighted, in copper-peach, with yellow-green throat. Tetraploid.

'Newton's Apple'–1985 (Elliott). Semievergreen. 19 in. Midseason. An interesting, 4½ in., light Cardinal-red, with chalky light colored eye zone, with blue highlights above the green throat. Diploid.

'Night Raider'–1981 (Webster). Dormant. 28 in. Midseason. A fine, 5½ in., bright, dark red self, with small green throat. Tetraploid.

'Night Raider'. Photo by WEBSTER

'Notorious'–1983 (Munson). Dormant. 24 in. Early midseason. Large, bright tomato-red, with large yellow-green throat. Tetraploid.

'Palace Guard'–1976 (Munson). Dormant. 28 in. Midseason. 5½ in., medium-large, wide petaled, full formed, brilliant, velvety, Chinese-red, with yellow throat. Tetraploid.

'Papal Guard'–1978 (Munson). Dormant. 24 in. Midseason late. 5½ in., extremely heavy substance, rose-red self, small, lemon-lime-green throat. Tetraploid.

'Pardon Me'–1982 (Apps). Dormant. 18 in. Midseason. 2¾ in., bright red self, with yellow-green throat. Miniature. Diploid.

'Pirate Lord'–1982 (Munson). Evergreen. 30 in. Early midseason. 5 in., full, flat, broad, shimmering rose-coral-red self, with yellow throat. Tetraploid.

'Pixie Pirate'–1986 (Elizabeth Hudson Salter). Semievergreen. 16 in. Midseason to late. A super, 3 in., bright cherry-red self, with yellow-green heart. Diploid.

'Post Time'–1972 (Wild). Dormant. 28 in. Early midseason. A round, overlapped, 5 in., ruby-red self, with lemon-yellow throat. A milestone and a classic. Diploid.

'Prime Minister'–1980 (Munson). Dormant. 28 in. Midseason. Medium to large, 5 in., broad, full, brilliant orange-red self, with small, yellow-green throat. Tetraploid.

'Principal Wife'–1986 (Weston). Semievergreen. 27 in. Midseason. Wonderfully formed, 4¾ in., red self, with yellow-green throat. Tetraploid.

'Principal Wife'. Photo by WESTON

'Rahotep'–1976 (Moldovan). Semievergreen. 26 in. Midseason late. Special, 5 in., rose-red self, with yellow throat. Tetraploid.

'Ram Chand'–1984 (Elliott). Semievergreen. 25 in. Midseason. Wonderfully formed, flat, and ruffled, 4½ in., claret and burgundy blend, with dark burgundy eye zone, and wide, green throat. Diploid.

'Reckless'–1986 (Varner). Dormant. 30 in. Midseason. A fine, 5½ in., medium deep

'Reckless'. Photo by VARNER

red, with wirelike, gold edges and very green throat. Tetraploid.

'Red Dog Two'–1977 (Harris). Dormant. 29 in. Midseason. 6½ in., large, tailored, full, overlapped, red self, with a darker halo, and green throat. Tetraploid.

'Red Mystique'–1987 (Peck). Dormant. 24 in. Midseason. 5 in., dark red, ruffled, self. Tetraploid.

'Red Mystique'. Photo by PECK

'Red Red Rose'–1982 (Moldovan). Dormant. 24 in. Midseason. Sunfast, ruffled, and overlapped, 5 in., cerise-red blend, with gold-green throat. Tetraploid.

'Red Rhapsody'–1981 (Peck). Dormant. 20 in. Midseason. 6 in., large, ruffled, bright red self, with green throat. Tetraploid.

'Red Tart'–1986 (Peck). Dormant. 20 in. Midseason. 5 in., bright red self, with green throat. Tetraploid.

'Red Volunteer'–1984 (Oakes). Dormant. 30 in. Midseason. 7 in., large, clear candle-red self, gold-yellow throat. Tetraploid.

'Richard Connelley'–1980 (Peck). Dormant. 24 in. Midseason. Full form, overlapped, 6 in., medium-large, rich, dark, ruffled, red self, with green heart. Tetraploid.

'Richard Taylor'–1987 (Munson). Semievergreen. 26 in. Midseason. Quite ruffled, 6½ in., bold, rich, red self, with deeper red highlights, and small, yellow-green throat and green heart. Tetraploid.

'Royal Exchequer'–1986 (Munson). Dormant. 24 in. Midseason. Broad, full formed, delicately ruffled, 5 in., bold shimmering red, with a small red-gold-green throat. Tetraploid.

'Ruby Throat'–1979 (Griesbach-Klehm). Dormant. 21 in. Midseason to late. Smooth, tailored, 5 in., red self. A special color. Tetraploid.

'Russell Southall'–1985 (Elliott). Semievergreen. 22 in. Midseason. Very fine, 5 in., dark cardinal-red and rose blend, with green throat. Diploid.

'Russell Southall'. Photo by ELLIOTT

'Saucy Rogue'–1984 (Elizabeth Hudson Salter). Semievergreen. 16 in. Midseason. A fine, 1¾ in., rose-red, with deeper red eye zone, and small, green throat. Diploid.

'Scarlet Chalice'–1984 (Munson). Semievergreen. 26 in. Midseason. 5½ in., large, flat, round, and bold, ruffled, brilliant scarlet-red self, with small, yellow-green throat. Tetraploid.

'Scarlock'–1974 (Peck). Dormant. 30 in. Early midseason. Classic, 6½ in., large, red self, with yellow-green throat. Tetraploid.

'Seductor'–1983 (Gates). Evergreen. 18 in. Early. 6 in. broad, full, overlapped, rich apple-red self, with large, bright lime-chartreuse throat. Tetraploid.

'Siloam Grace Stamile'–1984 (R. Henry). Dormant. 14 in. Early midseason. Superb, 2⅞ in., red self, with deeper red eye zone, and green throat. Diploid.

'Siloam Grace Stamile'. Photo by HENRY

'Siloam Helpmate'–1979 (R. Henry). Dormant. 25 in. Midseason. 4¼ in., small, red self, with green throat. Diploid.

'Siloam Jim Cooper'–1981 (R. Henry). Dormant. 16 in. Early midseason. 3½ in., round, full, small, rich, copper-red, with a bold, red eye zone, and green throat. A classic. Diploid.

'Siloam Jim Cooper'. Photo by HENRY

'Siloam Red Cherry'–1982 (R. Henry). Dormant. 22 in. Midseason. 3½ in., small, round, fully formed, red self, with green throat. Diploid.

'Siloam Red Ruby'–1977 (R. Henry). Dormant. 18 in. Midseason. 4 in., small, round, ruffled, velvet, red self, with small, green throat. Diploid.

'Siloam Red Toy'–1975 (R. Henry). Dormant. 20 in. Early midseason. 2¾ in., miniature, round, red self, with strong yellow-green throat. Diploid.

'Siloam Red Velvet'–1975 (R. Henry). Dormant. 26 in. Midseason. 5½ in., red self, with green throat. Diploid.

'Sir Lancelot'–1987 (Webster). Dormant. 26 in. Midseason. Superb, 5½ in., lightly ruffled, bright red self, with green throat. Holds well in hot weather. Tetraploid.

'Sir Lancelot'. Photo by WEBSTER

'Sir Wilford'–1985 (Yancey). Semievergreen. 26 in. Midseason. 5 in., rose-cherry-red blend, with light green throat. Greenish white darts, from the throat, a faint lavender-red watermark. Diploid.

'Sir Wilford'. Photo by YANCEY

'Sister McDuffie'–1985 (Durio). Evergreen. 30 in. Early midseason. 6½ in., rich, mahogany-red self, with bright chartreuse throat. Tetraploid.

'Sister McDuffie'. Photo by DURIO

'Slowly Won'–1973 (Peck). Dormant. 20 in. Early midseason. 6½ in., large, broad petaled, crimson-red self, with small, green throat. Tetraploid.

'Smoking Gun'–1987 (Peck). Dormant. 24 in. Midseason. New, medium-large, 5½ in., near black self, with yellow, star points radiating from green throat. Tetraploid.

'Stop Sign'–1984 (Millikan). Semievergreen. 28 in. Midseason late. 5½ in., fully formed, bright, rich, dark red, with green throat. Tetraploid.

'Smoking Gun'. Photo by PECK

'Timeless Fire'. Photo by GUIDRY

'Time Lord'. Photo by MUNSON

'Sultans Ruby'–1981 (Munson). Dormant. 24 in. Midseason late. 5 in., round, broad, full, and chalice-shaped, rich, garnet and ruby-red, with strong green throat. Tetraploid.

'Tallyman'–1979 (Moldovan). Dormant. 30 in. Midseason. 7 in., large, coral-red blend, with green-yellow throat. Tetraploid

'Three Diamonds'–1986 (Oscie B. Whatley). Dormant. 27 in. Midseason. Large, 6 in., dark red, with bold, green-chartreuse throat pattern. Tetraploid.

'Three Diamonds'. Photo by WHATLEY

'Timeless Fire'–1986 (Guidry). Evergreen. 18 in. Early midseason. 5¼ in., deep red self. Yellow-green throat. Diploid.

'Time Lord'–1983 (Munson). Evergreen. 30 in. Early midseason. 6 in., electric rose-red and copper blend, with violet highlights, and a lighter, bold eye, and large green throat. Tetraploid.

'Toy Troubador'–1984 (Elizabeth Hudson Salter). Evergreen. 16 in. Midseason. A handsome, 2¾ in., intense rose-red self, with a velvety texture, and bright green throat. Diploid.

'Velvet Promise'–1987 (Elizabeth Hudson Salter). Semievergreen. 22 in. Midseason. Superb, 3¼ in., rose-red self, with deeper red eye zone, and green throat. Diploid.

'Vintage Bordeaux'–1986 (Kirchhoff). Evergreen. 27 in. Early. 5¾ in., black-cherry, edged yellow, with chartreuse throat. Diploid.

'Wally Nance'–1976 (Wild). Dormant. 25 in. Early midseason. 6 in., large, broad, ruffled, ruby-red self, with small, strong, green throat. Diploid.

'War March'–1974 (Munson). Semievergreen. 30 in. Midseason. 5 in., broad, full, round, rather tailored, rich, burgundy to claret-red self, with yellow-green heart. Tetraploid.

'Vintage Bordeaux'. Photo by KIRCHHOFF

'Wayne Johnson'. Photo by BETTY HUDSON

'Warrior Prince'–1985 (Munson). Dormant. 5½ in. rich, bright or Chinese-red, with small, yellow throat and green heart. Tetraploid.

'Wayne Johnson'–1984 (Betty Hudson). Evergreen. 28 in. Midseason. 5½ in., large, broad petaled, ruffled, double flower of brilliant cerise-cherry-red, with green-gold heart. Tetraploid.

'When I Dream'–1979 (Yancey). Semi-evergreen. 28 in. Early midseason. 6½ in., large, blood-red self, with very large, yellow-green throat. Diploid.

'Wicked Witch'–1980 (Moldovan). Dormant. 24 in. Midseason. Small, deep maroon-red self, with green throat. Tetraploid.

'Wild Enchantress'–1984 (Elizabeth Hudson Salter). Evergreen. 18 in. Early midseason. Bold, 2½ in., enchanting flower of bright red-orange, with gold-green throat and gold midribs. Diploid.

PINK (PASTEL CREAM-PINK THROUGH DEEP ROSE)

'Adele McKinney'–1977 (Monette). Evergreen. 16 in. Early. 6½ in., pink self with green throat. Diploid.

'Allafrill'–1983 (Peck). Dormant. 28 in. Midseason. Large, 6 in., very ruffled, elegant, apricot-pink self, with yellow-green throat. Superb ruffling. Tetraploid.

'Angelotti'–1985 (J. Williams). Evergreen. 23 in. Early. A voluptuous, overlapped, 4 in. peach blend, with strong apricot throat. A superb jewel. Diploid.

'Anne McNutt'–1976 (Tanner). Evergreen. 24 in. Early midseason. Large, 6 in., pink self with lavender cast and green throat. Diploid.

'Antique Rose'–1987 (Sikes). Semievergreen. 25 in. Midseason. 5½ in., rose-pink blend, with ruffles and flutes, and yellow-green throat. Very fine. Diploid.

'Antique Rose'. Photo by SIKES

'Arpeggio'–1978 (Kirchhoff). Semievergreen. 20 in. Midseason. 5¼ in., pale coral-pink, ivory and cream blend, with green throat. A landmark double. Diploid.

'**Avon Crystal Rose**'–1981 (Moldovan). Dormant. 26 in. Midseason. 5½ in., rose-pink, with white watermark, and small greenish yellow throat. Clear and unique coloration. Tetraploid.

'**Ballet Music**'–1984 (Munson). Evergreen. 18 in. Midseason to late. A 4½ in., round, flat, and very ruffled and fluted, pale pink to rose-pink, with a light cream-lemon eye zone and chartreuse-green throat. Super bedding plant. Tetraploid.

'**Barbara Mitchell**'–1984 (Pierce). Semievergreen. 20 in. Midseason. 6 in., opulent pale pink, with narrow pink eye band, and a green throat. Diploid.

'Barbara Mitchell'. Photo by SIKES

'**Bathsheba**'–1983 (Harris-Benz). Evergreen. 25 in. Early midseason. Large, 6 in., pink self, with orchid highlights and a green throat. One of the much-discussed new daylilies. Tetraploid.

'**Becky Lynn**'–1977 (Guidry). Semievergreen. 20 in. Extra early. 6¾ in., lovely rose blend, of great clarity, with strong, green throat. Diploid.

'Becky Lynn'. Photo by GUIDRY

'**Bed of Clouds**'–1987 (Kirchhoff). Evergreen. 26 in. Early midseason. Pristine and elegant, 4¾ in. double of palest pink with yellow-green throat. Diploid.

'Bed of Clouds'. Photo by KIRCHHOFF

'**Beguiling Belle**'–1982 (Elizabeth Hudson Salter). Evergreen. 16 in. Midseason. A 2¾ in., smooth, pale salmon-pink self, of full, round, overlapped form. Throat is a deeper salmon, with a tiny, olive-green throat. Diploid.

'**Beijing**'–1986 (Munson). Evergreen. 24 in. Midseason. A 5 in., pale flesh-pink, with broad, voluptuous form and opulent ruffling, with small, cream-green throat. Superb in all facets. Tetraploid.

'Beijing'. Photo by MUNSON

'**Bird's Eye**'–1985 (Kirchhoff). Evergreen. 20 in. Extra early. 3½ in., ivory-cream with rose eye zone and green throat. Beguiling and unique. Diploid.

'**Bobbie Gerold**'–1980 (Graham). Evergreen. 26 in. Early. 5 in., double, pale salmon-apricot-pink self with yellow throat. Splendid form and lovely ruffling. Diploid.

'**Booger**'–1985 (Durio). Evergreen. 26 in. Early midseason. Large, 6½ in., baby-ribbon-pink with faint rouging, and a green throat. Form is broad and ruffled. Tetraploid.

'Bird's Eye'. Photo by KIRCHHOFF

'Booger'. Photo by DURIO

'Bookmark'. Photo by MUNSON

'Bookmark'–1982 (Munson). Evergreen. 24 in. Early midseason. 5 in., salmon-pink-beige self, with yellow-green throat. Broad, flat, and voluptuous. Tetraploid.

'Cajun Lady'–1985 (Guidry). Evergreen. 35 in. Extra early. Large, 6 in., rich salmon-rose and bronze blend, with green-gold throat. Form is broad, full, ruffled and recurved. Diploid.

'Cajun Lady'. Photo by GUIDRY

'Carefree Beauty'–1982 (Pierce). Semi-evergreen. 24 in. Midseason. 6½ in., pink self, with green throat. Diploid.

'Carman Marie'–1975 (Durio). Evergreen. 26 in. Early midseason. Broad, round, ruffled, large, 6½ in., rose-pink with deeper veining and green throat. A milestone. Diploid.

'Carman Marie'. Photo by DURIO

'Cee Tee'–1979 (Durio). Evergreen. 25 in. Early midseason. Large, full formed, 6½ in., clear, fresh pink with darker edges and green-yellow throat. Tetraploid.

'Chantelle'–1988 (Millikan). Semievergreen. 26 in. Late. 5½ in., medium pink with white midribs. Diploid.

'Cherry Chapeau'–1983 (Munson). Evergreen. 30 in. Early midseason. A 5 in., superb bicolor, with wide, round, broad, heavily ruffled and fluted form. Color is a

'Chantelle'. Photo by MILLIKAN

'Cherry Chapeau'. Photo by MUNSON

bright rose and flesh-cream. Petals strongly overlap sepals, allowing the rose coloring of the petals to form a complete circle throat, with a dark olive-chartreuse heart. Tetraploid.

'Chorus Line'–1981 (Kirchhoff). Evergreen. 20 in. Early. 3½ in., medium pink, with rose band above yellow halo, and dark green throat. Diploid.

'Classy Mama'–1987 (Peck). Dormant. 26 in. Midseason. Large, 6 in., heavily ruffled, cream, apricot-pink blend, with yellow-green throat. A class act. Tetraploid.

'Classy Mama'. Photo by PECK

'Coral Moon'–1983 (Munson). Evergreen. 28 in. Early midseason. 5 in., large, round, flat, voluptuous, lightly ruffled pastel coral, with pinkish highlights. Throat is circular, yellow-chartreuse. Tetraploid.

'Dance Ballerina Dance'–1976 (Peck). Dormant. 24 in., Midseason. Round, ruffled, and frilled, 6 in., apricot-pink self, with orange-pink throat. Not always perfectly formed, but always a show stopper. A milestone, and perhaps the most used tetraploid in breeding during the past seven years. Tetraploid.

'Dancing Shiva'–1974 (Moldovan). Dormant. 22 in. Early. 5 in., medium, pink blend, with green-yellow throat. Tetraploid.

'Davis Guidry'–1985 (Guidry). Evergreen. 26 in. Early. Bold, 6 in., cinnamon-pink blend, with olive-green throat. Unique. Diploid.

'Davis Guidry'. Photo by GUIDRY

'Deezee'–1987 (Albert Durio). Dormant. 20 in. Midseason. 6 in., ruffled, hot coral-pink, with gold throat. Tetraploid.

'Deezee'. Photo by DURIO

67

'Delightsome'–1985 (Sikes). Semievergreen. 16 in. Midseason. 4¾ in., very ruffled, rich pink self, with yellow-green throat. Diploid.

'Delightsome'. Photo by SIKES

'Diva Assoluta'–1985 (Morss). Semievergreen. 26 in. Midseason. Large, 6 in., cream-pink, touched pink, with yellow edge and green throat. Special. Tetraploid.

'Diva Assoluta'. Photo by MORSS

'Double Conch Shell'–1987 (Stamile). Evergreen. 26 in. Early midseason. 6 in., double, cream-melon-pink, with yellow-green throat. Uniquely formed, and very beautiful. Diploid.

'Double Conch Shell'. Photo by STAMILE

'Double Pink Treasure'–1981 (E. C. Brown). Semievergreen. 21 in. Early midseason. 6 in., double, medium pink self, with green throat. Handsome double. Diploid.

'Dream Awhile'–1981 (E. C. Brown). Semievergreen. 23 in. Early midseason. 5½ in., clear soft pink self, with green throat. Diploid.

'Dream Awhile'. Photo by BROWN, E.C.

'Elsie Spalding'–1985 (W. M. Spalding). Evergreen. 14 in. Midseason. Voluptuous, 6 in., ivory blushed pink, with light russet-pink halo, and strong green throat. Quietly elegant, and genuinely superb. Diploid.

'Enchanted Empress'–1980 (Munson). Evergreen. 30 in. Midseason late. Broad, full, flat, 6 in., pale ivory-cream-pink self, with cream-green heart. Superb scapes, and impeccable branching. Tetraploid.

'Enchanting Blessing'–1983 (W. M. Spalding). Evergreen. 19 in. Midseason. 5½ in., peach-pink blend, with green throat. Diploid.

'Fairy Tale Pink'–1980 (Pierce). Semievergreen. 24 in. Midseason. 5½ in., pale pink self, with green heart. Lovely form. Diploid.

'Frank Gladney'–1979 (Durio). Evergreen. 26 in. Early midseason. Round, opu-

'Frank Gladney'. Photo by DURIO

lent, 6½ in., hot coral-cerise self with gold throat. Special. Tetraploid.

'Frills and Lace'–1987 (Stamile). Dormant. 26 in. Midseason late. 5½ in., apricot-pink blend, with orange-green throat. Tetraploid.

'Frills and Lace'. Photo by STAMILE

'Frosted Pink Ice'–1987 (Stamile). Dormant. 28 in. Midseason. Round, ruffled, overlapped, 5 in., bluish pink self with white midribs and yellow-green throat. Sensational. Diploid.

'Frosted Pink Ice'. Photo by STAMILE

'Geppetto'–1986 (Moldovan). Dormant. 26 in. Early. Voluptuous, overlapped, 5 in. pink-cream, with strong pink eye zone, and

'Geppetto'. Photo by MOLDOVAN

yellow-green throat. Elegant. Tetraploid.

'Hail Mary'–1984 (Moldovan). Dormant. 24 in. Early. Superb, 5½ in. pink blend, with silver highlights, with subtle pink halo, and lemon watermark, above yellow-green throat. A milestone in pink breeding. Tetraploid.

'Hatteras'–1981 (Sellers). Semievergreen. 26 in. Midseason. 5 in. pink self, with green throat. Diploid.

'Hazel Monette'–1973 (Monette). Evergreen. 22 in. Early midseason. Large, broad, flat, 6 in., pale pink self, with green throat. Diploid.

'Hester'–1987 (Millikan). Semievergreen. 26 in. Midseason. 5½ in., round, ruffled, and overlapped, deep rose-cerise self with deep green throat. Diploid.

'Hester'. Photo by MILLIKAN

'Imperial Treasure'–1983 (Munson). Evergreen. 26 in. Early midseason. Elegant, large, 6 in. coral-pink, with yellow-green throat. Tetraploid.

'Janice Brown'–1986 (E. C. Brown). Semievergreen. 21 in. Early midseason. Round, full, flat, and superb, medium, 4¼ in. bright pink, with rose-pink eye zone, and green throat. Diploid.

'Janice Brown'. Photo by BROWN, E.C.

'Kate Carpenter'–1980 (Munson). Evergreen. 28 in. Early midseason. 6 in. pale cream-pink blend, with cream-green throat. Superb in every way. A classic. Tetraploid.

'Kenya'–1982 (Durio). Semievergreen. 26 in. Early. Large, flat, triangular, 7 in., flesh-pink blend, with moss-green throat. Tetraploid.

'Lauren Leah'–1983 (Pierce). Dormant. 18 in. Early midseason. Creamy pink blend, with green throat. Diploid.

'Lauren Leah'. Photo by SIKES

'Little Brandy'–1979 (Guidry). Evergreen. 20 in. Extra Early. Broad, full, round, 5 in. pale pink blend, with green throat. Diploid.

'Little Isaac'–1987 (Durio). Dormant. 26 in. Early midseason. 5 in., broad, round, formed pink blend, with coral-pink knobbies on ruffled petal, and sepal edges, with green heart. Tetraploid.

'Little Issac'. Photo by DURIO

'Little Pink Umbrella'–1985 (Cruse). Evergreen. 18 in. Early midseason. Small, 3½ in., round, full and overlapped, pale pink self, with green throat. A jewel. Diploid.

'London Lady'–1985 (Elizabeth Hudson Salter). Evergreen. 18 in. Midseason to late. Round, overlapped, full, 3 in., bright clear rose-pink, with tiny yellow-green heart. Diploid.

'Love Goddess'–1979 (Moldovan). Dormant. 26 in. Early. 5 in., strong rose-pink, with amber edges, and green throat. Extraordinary. Tetraploid.

'Lyric Serenade'–1984 (Munson). Evergreen. 20 in. Early midseason. Large, 5 in., salmon-pink, of chalice form highlighted by a yellow-green throat. Tetraploid.

'Mariska'–1984 (Moldovan). Dormant. 28 in. Midseason. Broad, full, flat, large, 6 in., pale pink, with orchid undertones and lemon-green throat. Very elegant. Tetraploid.

'Martha Adams'–1979 (W. Spalding). Evergreen. 19 in. Early midseason. Large, flat, voluptuous, 6 in., pink self, of great clarity, with green throat. One of the finest. Diploid.

'Mary Mae Simon'–1965 (MacMillan). Evergreen. 32 in. Early. 5¼ in., cream-pink blend, with green throat. Special. Diploid.

'Mavis Smith'–1974 (Lenington). Semievergreen. 33 in. Midseason. 5 in., pale cream flushed pink, of gorgeous form, and a green throat. Top drawer. Diploid.

'Merry Witch'–1983 (Munson). Evergreen. 30 in. Midseason. 6 in., multiblend of magenta-rose, rose and rose-pink, with a lighter eye of chalky-rose, and a round, lemon-chartreuse throat. Unique and very special. Tetraploid.

'Ming Porcelain'–1981 (Kirchhoff). Evergreen. 28 in. Early. 5¼ in., pastel ivory-pink, touched peach, edged gold, and wide, yellow halo, with lime-green throat. Very special pastel pink. Tetraploid.

'Ming Porcelain'. Photo by KIRCHHOFF

'Moonlight Mist'–1981 (Elizabeth Hudson Salter). Evergreen. 18 in. Midseason. 3 in., small, palest ivory and cream-pink with a chartreuse heart. One of the finest. Diploid.

'Moon Twilight'–1977 (Munson). Evergreen. 24 in. Early midseason. Large, broad petaled, 5 in., bright pale pink, of clear coloration, with large, cream-white throat, and a chartreuse heart. Tetraploid.

'Myrtle McKneeley'–1986 (Dalton Durio). Evergreen. 25 in. Midseason. Large, 6 in., ruffled cream, with pink tints, and chartreuse throat. Tetraploid.

'Myrtle McKneeley'. Photo by DURIO

'Neal Berrey'–1985 (Sikes). Diploid. 18 in. Midseason. 5 in., lush ruffled, rose-pink blend, with green-yellow throat. Super form and color blending. Diploid.

'Neal Berrey'. Photo by SIKES

'Palace Lantern'–1978 (Munson). Evergreen. 26 in. Midseason. 6 in., bright rose-pink blend, with gold-lime throat. Tetraploid.

'Pa Pa Gulino'–1977 (Durio). Semievergreen. 26 in. Early. 6 in., double, silvery flesh-pink with rose rouge above a citron-green throat. Tetraploid.

'Pa Pa Gulino'. Photo by DURIO

'Petite Pastel Princess'–1985 (Elizabeth Hudson Salter). Evergreen. 15 in. Midseason to late. Full, round, and overlapped, 2½ in., blend and shadings of peach, apricot, and pink. Pale lilac midribs, and olive-green heart. Diploid.

'Pink Corduroy'–1984 (Stamile). Semievergreen. 28 in. Midseason. 5½ in., rich, fragrant, pink, with light chartreuse throat. Diploid.

'Pink Corduroy'. Photo by STAMILE

'Pink Monday'–1981 (Sellers). Dormant. 26 in. Midseason. Fully formed, 5½" pale rose-pink self, with green throat. Special. Tetraploid.

'Pink Salute'–1987 (Millikan). Semievergreen. 26 in. Midseason to late. Opulent, large, 6 in., ruffled, salmon-rose-pink self, with green throat. Beautiful form, and style. Diploid.

'Pink Salute'. Photo by MILLIKAN

'Premier Rose'. Photo by MUNSON

'Pink Thistledown'–1986 (Millikan). Semievergreen. 25 in. Midseason. Superb, 5 in. apple-blossom-pink self, with yellow-green throat. Form and color exemplary. Diploid.

'Pleated Gown'–1976 (Peck). Dormant. 28 in. Midseason. 6 in. apricot-pink and yellow polychrome, with green-yellow throat. Tetraploid.

'Poogie'–1978 (Peck). Dormant. 19 in. Midseason. 5 in. pink self, with green-yellow throat. Tetraploid.

'Poult-de-Soie'–1986 (Woodhall). Dormant. 26 in. Early. 5½ in. shrimp-pink blend, with very large, green-lime throat. Tetraploid.

'Regency Rosette'–1987 (Elizabeth Hudson Salter). Semievergreen. 20 in. Midseason to late. Heavy substance and lightly ruffled, full, round, overlapped, 2¾ in., bright rose-pink, with green-gold heart. Diploid.

'Poult-de-Soie'. Photo by WOODHALL

'Regency Rosette'. Photo by SALTER

'Premier Rose'–1983 (Munson). Evergreen. 22 in. Early midseason. Medium-large, 5 in., bright pink-salmon-rose, of full, and overlapped form. Throat is green-gold with lime heart. Substance is heavy, waxy and sun resistant. Tetraploid.

'Rainbow Round'–1984 (Moldovan). Dormant. 28 in. Midseason. 6 in. rose-pink, edged gold, with cream-pink watermark, and green-yellow throat. Tetraploid.

'Robbie Salter'–1982 (Kirchhoff). Evergreen. 24 in. Midseason. 3¼ in., clear, medium coral-pink, edged buff, with deeper coral band, above green throat. Diploid.

'Rose Emily'–1982 (Pierce). Semievergreen. 18 in. Midseason. 5 in., rose self, with green throat. Diploid.

'Rose Swan'–1978 (W. Spalding). Evergreen. 22 in, Midseason. 6½ in., rose self, with green throat. Diploid.

'Round Table'–1974 (Peck). Dormant. 32 in. Midseason. 5½ in., pink blend, with green-yellow throat. Tetraploid.

'Sean Alexander'–1983 (Pierce). Semievergreen. 18 in. Early midseason. 6 in., pink self, with green throat. Diploid.

'Selma Timmons'–1987 (Munson). Semievergreen. 18 in. Early midseason. This 4½ in., small, full, flower with diminutive ruffles, is pink-persimmon, with deeper pink highlights, and tiny, round, greenish gold throat. Substance is heavy, and color tones more pink in the sun. Grand. Tetraploid.

'Selma Timmons'. Photo by MUNSON

'Sherry Fair'–1978 (Peck). Dormant. 24 in. Midseason. 6 in., rose-pink self, with green throat. Special Color. Tetraploid.

'Shibui Splendor'–1974 (Munson). Evergreen. 24 in. Early midseason. Large, handsome, 6 in., cream-pink self, with chartreuse throat. Grand in every way. Diploid.

'Siloam Angelic Love'–1987 (R. Henry). Dormant. 20 in. Early midseason. 3¾ in., cream pale pink blend, with green throat. Special and pristine. Diploid.

'Siloam Angelic Love'. Photo by HENRY

'Siloam Apple Blossom'–1983 (R. Henry). Dormant. 18 in. Early midseason. 3¾ in., pink self, with green throat. Breathtaking. Diploid.

'Siloam Apple Blossom'. Photo by HENRY

'Siloam Double Dumpy'–1986 (R. Henry). Dormant. 18 in. Midseason. 5½ in., bold, double pink blend, with green throat. Unique. Diploid.

'Silver Ice'–1983 (Munson). Evergreen. 28 in. Midseason to late. Large, 6 in., broadly formed, wide spread, flat, impeccably clear, ice pink, blushed with a silver or palest lilac tint. The throat is palest chartreuse and blends subtly with the pale petal color. Color frosts in the sun. Tetraploid.

'Smoky Mountain Autumn'–1986 (Guidry). Dormant. 18 in. Early. 5¾ in., copper-rose blend, with rose-lavender halo and yellow-green throat. Beguiling color. Diploid.

'Smoky Mountain Autumn'. Photo by GUIDRY

'Smooth Flight'–1981 (Peck). Dormant. 28 in. Midseason. 6 in., pink self, with green-yellow throat. Tetraploid.

'Someone Special'–1985 (Sikes). Dormant. 26 in. Midseason. 5 in., delicate pink self, green radiates from the throat turning to pale yellow as it is overlaid by a very deep pink halo. Diploid.

'Someone Special'. Photo by SIKES

'Southern Charmer'–1983 (Sikes). Evergreen. 26 in. Midseason. 5 in. rose self, with green-yellow throat. Diploid.

'Southern Love'–1985 (Sikes). Dormant. 30 in., Midseason. 5½ in. flesh-pink, ruffled, self with chartreuse throat that radiates onto the petals. Diploid.

'Southern Love'. Photo by SIKES

'Spring Muslin'–1986 (Elizabeth Hudson Salter). Evergreen. 20 in. Midseason. Round, full, tailored, 3½ in., soft rose-pink, with chartreuse heart. Diploid.

'Spode'–1984 (Munson). Evergreen. 36 in. Midseason to late. Elegant, 6 in., crisp, waxlike, pale pink, shaded in palest hues of ivory-flesh and pink, with a pale ivory-chartreuse throat. A tiny gold thread is present on the flowers' delicate ruffles. Tetraploid.

'Strawberry Rose'–1980 (Peck). Dormant. 27 in. Midseason. 6½ in., rose-pink self, with green throat. Tetraploid.

'Tani'–1983 (Pierce). Semievergreen. 24 in. Early midseason. Opulent, large, 6 in.,

'Tani'. Photo by JOHNSON

very light rose-pink self, with green throat. Diploid.

'Tropical Doll'–1983 (Guidry). Evergreen. 20 in. Midseason. 6 in., ruffled, cream color, with a pink blush, and diamond dusting. Diploid.

'Tropical Doll'. Photo by GUIDRY

'Vera Biaglow'–1984 (Moldovan). Dormant. 28 in. Midseason late. A magnificent, large, 6 in., rose-pink, edged ivory-silver, with lemon-green throat. Form is full, opulent, and lightly ruffled. Exceptional in every way. Tetraploid.

'Windermere'–1978 (J. Williams). Evergreen. 22 in. Midseason. Superb, 6 in., pale pink-beige blend, with large, cream-yellow throat. Form is full, round and very flat. Special. Diploid.

'Winnie'–1978 (Durio). Evergreen. 26 in. Early midseason. Handsome 5½ in., shell-pink, veined coral, with gold edges, and green-yellow throat. Tetraploid.

'Yazoo Johnny Hughes'–1983 (W. H. Smith). Semievergreen. 20 in. Early midseason. 5½ in., elegant, ruffled, cream-yellow and pink blend double, with chartreuse heart. Handsome. Diploid.

'Winnie'. Photo by DURIO

'Yazoo Mildred Primos'. Photo by SMITH

'Yazoo Johnny Hughes'. Photo by SMITH

'Yazoo Souffle'. Photo by SMITH

'Yazoo Mildred Primos'–1984 (W. H. Smith). Semievergreen. 26 in. Midseason. 4 in., round, full, lightly ruffled, flesh-pink, with chartreuse throat. Diploid.

'Yazoo Souffle'–1983 (W. H. Smith). Semievergreen. 26 in. Early midseason. 5½ in., ruffled, classic double, of light apricot-pink cream, with a chartreuse throat. Special. Diploid.

PURPLE (PURPLE THROUGH BLACK-RED)

'Apollodorus'–1984 (Munson). Evergreen. 28 in. Midseason to late. Rich, medium-small, 4½ in. violet-purple with small, green throat, that radiates into petal color forming a lighter eye zone. Tetraploid.

'Black Watch'–1976 (Barrere). Dormant. 25 in. Early midseason. 6 in., deep burgundy self, with yellow-green throat. Tetraploid.

'Brent Gabriel'–1981 (Guidry). Evergreen. 20 in. Extra early. 5½ in., double purple bitone, with white watermarks, and green throat. Diploid.

'Cairo Night'–1986 (Munson). Evergreen. 26 in. Early midseason. Bold, 6 in., rich black-red-purple, with chalky red-purple eye zone, with yellow-green throat. Superb. Tetraploid.

'Cairo Night'. Photo by MUNSON

'**Cameroons**'–1984 (Munson). Evergreen. 28 in. Midseason. 6 in. bold, broad petaled, ruffled, fluted, claret wine-purple, with a chalky pinkish wine eye, and lime-chartreuse throat. Tetraploid.

'Cameroons'. Photo by MUNSON

'**Catherine Neal**'–1981 (Jack Carpenter). Dormant. 30 in. Very late. Large, bold, 6 in. purple self, with vibrant green throat. Very fine. Diploid.

'**Chicago Pansy**'–1977 (Marsh). Semievergreen. 28 in., Early. 6 in., plum-purple blend, with darker eye zone and cream-green throat. Tetraploid.

'**Chicago Royal Robe**'–1978 (Marsh). Semievergreen. 25 in. Early. 5½ in., plum-purple self, with green throat. Tetraploid.

'**Concord Town**'–1979 (Moldovan). Dormant. 26 in. Midseason late. 5½, in. purple, with black eye zone and green-yellow throat. Very rich and darkly colored. Tetraploid.

'**Court Magician**'–1987 (Munson). Evergreen. 26 in. Midseason late. Round, ruffled, 5½ in., rich purple-lavender, with chalky lighter eye of whiteish lavender. Throat is large, bold, and yellow-green with a green heart. Very special. Tetraploid.

'**Damascan Velvet**'–1980 (Munson). Dormant. 22 in. Late. Large, broad petaled, rich, burgundy-violet purple self, with a small, chalky eye, and a strong yellow-green throat. Good form, broad and overlapped. Very striking. Very good substance. Tetraploid.

'**Damascene**'–1974 (Munson). Semievergreen. 30 in. Midseason. 5½ in., rose-lavender-mauve, with light blue-violet halo, and cream throat. Tetraploid.

'Court Magician'. Photo by MUNSON

'**Dark Dwarf**'–1984 (Elizabeth Hudson). Evergreen. 16 in. Midseason. 3¼ in., round, full formed, dark rose-red, with a bright yellow-green throat. Diploid.

'**Deep Pools**'–1979 (Yancey). Semievergreen. 20 in. Midseason. 6 in., bright orchid-purple shaded blue, with lavender-purple halo, and green-yellow throat. Diploid.

'**De Vaughn Hodges**'–1979 (Durio). Evergreen. 20 in. Early. 4½ in., double, Amaranth-rose, with ruby-red eye zone, and green throat. Tetraploid.

'De Vaughn Hodges'. Photo by DURIO

'**Doge of Venice**'–1982 (Munson). Evergreen. 28 in. Early midseason. Medium-large, broad petaled, 5 in. rich dark purple, flat and elegant, with silver-plum eye, and appliqued-like throat pattern of yellow-green. Tetraploid.

'**Dominic**'–1984 (J. Williams). Semievergreen. 30 in. Early midseason. Rich, 5½ in., dark black-red self, with light yellow throat. Tetraploid.

'**Double Grapette**'–1976 (Betty Brown). Evergreen. 24 in. Early. 4½ in., double, dark purple self, with green throat. Diploid.

'**Ed Murray**'–1971 (Grovatt). Dormant. 30 in. Midseason. Black-red self, with green throat. A classic. Diploid.

'**Empress Seal**'–1975 (Moldovan). Dormant. 28 in. Early midseason. 6 in., light orchid blend, with large chalk-white eye zone, and cream-green throat. Induced tetraploid.

'**Grand Masterpiece**'–1984 (Dove). Dormant. 21 in. Early midseason. Medium-large, 5¾ in., rich, deep purple self, with lime-green throat. Form, broad, full and ruffled. Diploid.

'**Grape Ripples**'–1983 (Carpenter-Glidden). Evergreen. 24 in. Midseason. Excellent, 5 in., grape-purple self, with green throat. Diploid.

'**Hamlet**'–1983 (Talbott). Dormant. 18 in. Early midseason. 5 in., medium-large, rich purple, with light blue-purple halo, and green throat. Full, flat form. Diploid.

'**Indigo Moon**'–1987 (Stamile). Dormant. 24 in. Early Midseason. Large, 6½ in., purple with green throat. Tetraploid.

'Indigo Moon'. Photo by STAMILE

'**Inez Sorrell**'–1986 (Dove). Dormant. 18 in. Midseason late. 5½ in., dark, rich, purple self, with lime-green throat. Form, wide, full, and flat. Diploid.

'**Jessica Lilian**'–1980 (Childs). Dormant. 26 in. Early midseason. Large, 6½ in., spidery purple, with darker eye zone and green throat. Diploid.

'**Khans Knight**'–1980 (Munson). Semievergreen. 24 in. Midseason late. 5 in., rich, velvety, black-purple, edged in ivory-white, with lime-chartreuse throat. Tetraploid.

'**Kurumba**'–1985 (J. Weston). Evergreen. 22 in. Early midseason. Large, 5½ in., broad, full, purple and mauve polychrome, edged in yellow, with patterned chartreuse throat. Tetraploid.

'Kurumba'. Photo by WESTON

'**Little Grapette**'–1970 (Williamson). Semievergreen. 12 in. Early. 2½ in., light grape-purple self. A classic. Diploid.

'**Loisteen Kirkman**'–1975 (Peck). Dormant. 27 in. Midseason. 6 in., light violet-purple self, with green throat. Tetraploid.

'**Lord Chamberlain**'–1984 (Moldovan). Dormant. 28 in. Midseason. 6 in., lavender-purple blend, shaded silver with yellow-amber watermark, and lemon-green throat. Extraordinary. Tetraploid.

'**Malaysian Monarch**'–1986 (Munson). Semievergreen. 24 in. Early midseason. Large, 6 in., bold, elegant, grape-purple, with large, round, creamy ivory-chartreuse throat. Tetraploid.

'Malaysian Monarch'. Photo by MUNSON

'**Midnight Magic**'–1979 (Kinnebrew). Evergreen. 28 in. Early midseason. Medium-large, 5½ in., broad, ruffled, black-red self, with green throat. Tetraploid.

'**Night Wings**'–1985 (J. Williams). Evergreen. 30 in. Early. Rich, 6 in., black-red self, with blue-black sheen, and yellow-green throat. Incredible. Tetraploid.

'**Nile Flower**'–1976 (Moldovan). Dormant. 26 in. Early midseason. Large, 6 in., vibrant claret-red-purple blend, with green-yellow throat. Tetraploid.

'**Nivia Guest**'–1990 (Munson). Evergreen. 24 in. Midseason. Medium-large, 5 in., deep wine-purple, with a lighter chalky eye zone and yellow-green throat. Tetraploid.

'Nivia Guest'. Photo by MUNSON

'**Old Port**'–1980 (Pride). Dormant. 29 in. Midseason. Large tailored, 7 in., wine-purple, with deep purple eye zone. Tetraploid.

'**Olive Bailey Langdon**'–1974 (Munson). Semievergreen. 28 in. Early midseason. Medium-large, 5 in., deep violet-purple, with yellow-green throat. A classic. Tetraploid.

'**Olivier Monette**'–1973 (Monette). Evergreen. 22 in. Early midseason. 6 in., wine-purple self, with yellow-green throat. Handsome form. Diploid.

'**Purple Arachne**'–1982 (Webster). 22 in. Dormant. Midseason. 7 in., dark purple spider, with a wide green shading to chartreuse throat. Tetraploid.

'**Respighi**'–1986 (Munson). 26 in. Evergreen. Early midseason. 6 in. wine-purple, with chalky-wine eye zone, and yellow-green throat. Tetraploid.

'**Royal Blue Blood**'–1979 (Hite). Dormant. 28 in. Early midseason. 5 in., deep bluish purple, with lighter bluish eye, and yellow-green throat. Special. Tetraploid.

'**Royal Heiress**'–1982 (Munson). Evergreen. 34 in. Early midseason. Large, bold, 6 in., round, full, rich burgundy-claret with chalky, circle eye, topping a chartreuse-yellow throat. Special. Tetraploid.

'**Royal Heritage**'–1978 (Munson). Semievergreen. 32 in. Midseason to late. A large, 6 in., violet-lavender, with a round throat of cream-yellow, that is prominent and extends into the petal color, forming a very distinct watermark, green heart. Tetraploid.

'**Royal Saracen**'–1982 (Munson). Evergreen. 28 in. Late midseason. Large, handsome, 6 in., lavender-purple, with a lighter lavender watermark, bordering a large, creamy chartreuse throat. Form is full, and ruffled. A milestone. Tetraploid.

'**Royal Viking**'–1978 (Hite). Semievergreen. 20 in. Early midseason. 6 in., burgundy-purple self, with green throat. Tetraploid.

'**Sebastian**'–1978 (J. Williams). Evergreen. 20 in. Early midseason. Medium-large, 5½ in. vivid light lavender-purple self, with lime-green throat. Superb in every way. Diploid.

'**Siamese Royalty**'–1980 (Munson). Semievergreen. 28 in. Early midseason. 5 in., broad, flat, ruffled, claret-wine to burgundy-rose. Throat is creamy green, small, round, and overlaps the petal color, to form a small watermark lighter eye. Unique. Tetraploid.

'**Stroke of Midnight**'–1981 (Kirchhoff). Evergreen. 25 in. Extra early. Bold, rich, 5 in., double Bordeaux-red self, with chartreuse throat. Scintillating. Diploid.

'**Strutter's Ball**'–1984 (Moldovan). Dormant. 28 in. Midseason. Elegant, 6 in., purple self, with very small silvery white watermark, above small, lemon-green throat. A milestone and an incredible achievement. Tetraploid.

'**Super Babe**'–1983 (Dove). Dormant. 19 in. Early midseason. Large, 6 in., broad, full, overlapped, black-purple self, with strong lime-green throat. Very impressive. Diploid.

'**Super Delight**'–1982 (Dove). Semievergreen. 18 in. Midseason late. 4¾ in., deep purple self, with lime-green throat. Diploid.

'**Super Medallion**'–1986 (Dove). Dormant. 24 in. Midseason late. Rich, 6½ in., purple-plum self, with lime-green throat. Bold, full form. Diploid.

'**Super Purple**'–1979 (Dove). Semievergreen. 27 in. Midseason. 5½ in., dark reddish purple self, with lime-green throat. Handsomely formed. Diploid.

'**Swirling Water**'–1978 (Carpenter). Semievergreen. 22 in. Early midseason. 6½ in., purple self, with cream-white splash, and green throat. Special. Diploid.

'**Tiffany Jeane**'–1980 (Childs). Dormant. 24 in. Midseason. 6 in., blue-purple self, with green throat. Very special color. Diploid.

'**Troubled Waters**'–1984 (Peck). Dormant. 20 in. Midseason. 6 in., quite dark, black-red-purple self, with green throat. Tetraploid.

'**Violet Hour**'–1978 (Peck). Dormant. 25 in. Midseason. 6½ in., violet-plum self, with green throat. Tetraploid.

'Zinfandel'–1980 (Kirchhoff). Evergreen. 26 in. Early. Bold, 6½ in., rich, wine self, with chartreuse throat. Handsome, full, form. Diploid.

LAVENDERS (MAUVE THROUGH LILAC)

'Alvatine Taylor'–1982 (Munson). Evergreen. 32 in. Early midseason. Large, 6 in., very broad, overlapped, blend of cream-pink, ivory-beige, lilac, and lavender-cream. Pale green throat. Excellent vigor, increases well. A classic. Tetraploid.

'Alvatine Taylor'. Photo by MUNSON

'Benchmark'–1980 (Munson). Evergreen. 30 in. Midseason. 6 in., unique, broad petaled, lavender self, with a shimmering, ivory-chartreuse and green throat. Tetraploid.

'Benchmark'. Photo by MUNSON

'Borgia Queen'–1986 (Munson). Evergreen. 26 in. Midseason to late. 5 in., silvery lavender-mauve, with a slate blue-violet eye zone, and cream-chartreuse throat. Tetraploid.

'Borgia Queen'. Photo by MUNSON

'Brandenburg'–1984 (Munson). Evergreen. 26 in. Early midseason. 6 in., broad petaled, pastel lilac-orchid, with a small, yellow-cream throat, and chartreuse heart. Tetraploid.

'Catherine Woodbery'–1967 (Childs). Dormant. 30 in. Midseason late. 6 in., pale orchid self, with green throat. A classic. Diploid.

'Diamond Shadows'–1983 (Munson). Semievergreen. 26 in. Early midseason. 5 in., broad petaled, flat lavender-slate self, with a lemon-cream throat and bright chartreuse heart. Tetraploid.

'Egyptian Ibis'–1984 (Munson). Evergreen. 24 in. Early midseason. 6 in., wide petaled, overlapped, but the form is not round, pale silver-pink-lilac, with a bright chartreuse throat. Tetraploid.

'Faberge'–1986 (Ida Munson). Semievergreen. 20 in. Midseason. A unique 4½ in., lavender-orchid-pink, edged yellow-gold, with a chalk-pink eye zone, and yellow-green throat. Tetraploid.

'Fancy Illusion'–1983 (Munson). Evergreen. 24 in. Early to early midseason. 5 in., broad, full, flat, and lightly ruffled, pale lilac and violet self, with chalky lilac eye zone, and bright green, circle heart, in a cream-yellow throat. Tetraploid.

'High Lama'–1978 (Munson). Evergreen. 30 in. Early midseason. 5 in., broad petaled, pale mauve-lavender self, with cream-green throat. Tetraploid.

'High Lama'. Photo by MUNSON

'Ida Wimberly Munson'–1979 (Munson). Semievergreen. 26 in. Midseason late. 6 in., opulent, pastel lilac-pink self, with cream-green throat. Tetraploid.

'Ida Wimberly Munson'. Photo by MUNSON

'Ilonka'–1984 (Moldovan). Dormant. 28 in. Midseason. 7 in., orchid-lavender blend, with silver-gray watermark, and yellow-green throat. Tetraploid.

'Ivory Dawn'–1982 (Munson). Semievergreen. 28 in. Midseason. 5 in., medium-large, slightly recurved, ivory-lavender, with pale lime-green throat. Tetraploid.

'Ivory Dawn'. Photo by MUNSON

'Nile Crane'–1978 (Munson). Evergreen. 26 in. Midseason. 5 in., medium-large, silver-lilac to bluish lavender, with highlights of cream-flesh and chartreuse, with cream throat. Tetraploid.

'Prince of Venice'–1983 (Munson). Evergreen. 30 in. Early midseason. 5 in., medium-large, rose-violet-mauve self, with broad, overlapping petals, and bright chartreuse throat. Tetraploid.

'Oueen's Memento'–1986 (Munson). Evergreen. 18 in. Midseason late. 6 in., medium-large, round, flat, ruffled, orchid-lavender self, with cream-yellow throat, chartreuse heart. Tetraploid.

'Sinbad Sailor'–1980 (Moldovan). Dormant. 28 in. Midseason. 5 in., medium-large, lavender self, with cream watermark. Tetraploid.

'Sovereign Queen'–1983 (Munson). Evergreen. 28 in. Late midseason. 6 in., large, broad petaled, pristine, lilac-pink, with an undertone of lavender, cream-chartreuse throat. Tetraploid.

'Winter Reverie'–1980 (Munson). Semievergreen. 20 in. Early midseason. 5 in., medium, pastel lavender-mauve, with cream-green throat. Tetraploid.

'**Bangkok Belle**'–1987 (Elizabeth Hudson Salter). Semidormant. 18 in. Midseason. A unique, 2½ in., round, full, overlapped, and lightly ruffled, rose-pink, with a gold eye pattern, above a round, green throat. Diploid.

'Bird Land'. Photo by KIRCHHOFF

'Bangkok Belle'. Photo by SALTER

'**Bette Davis Eyes**'–1982 (Kirchhoff). Evergreen. 23 in. Early. Handsome and exotic, 5¼ in., light lavender, with bold grape-purple eye zone, and intense lime-green throat. Diploid.

'**Bird Land**'–1987 (Kirchhoff). Evergreen. 24 in. Midseason. A 4 in., double of pastel amber-peach, with a medium coral-rose-red eye zone and a green throat. Very round, full and light ruffled. A very good double form. Diploid.

'**Bull Durham**'–1983 (Elliott). Semievergreen. 18 in. Early midseason. A 7 in., butter-yellow buff, with a large, magenta-purple eye zone and olive-green throat. Diploid.

'**Byzantine Mask**'–1983 (Munson). Evergreen. 26 in. Early midseason. 6 in., large, broad, overlapped, triangular formed silver-lavender, with a bold and stunning deeper eye of plum-purple and small, yellow-green throat. Tetraploid.

'**Caliph's Robe**'–1981 (Munson). Evergreen. 28 in. A medium-large, 6 in., wide petaled, rosy violet-plum, with a raisin-plum eye, and yellow-green throat. A wire-like, gold edge. Tetraploid.

'**Changeling**'–1983 (Elizabeth Hudson Salter). Semievergreen. 20 in. Midseason. A

'Bull Durham'. Photo by ELLIOTT

very different and unique, 3¼ in., reverse bicolor of palest pink and lavender-mauve, with a very distinct eye pattern of pale chalky lavender, highlighted by an outline of deep lavender-rose. Pale cream midribs extend from the lime throat ending at the eye zone outline. The sepals reflect deeper eye color of this eye within an eye. Diploid.

'**Chicago Picotee Queen**'–1976 (Marsh). Semievergreen. 20 in. Large, 6¼ in., light lilac-lavender, with bold eye of light plum-purple, and yellow-green throat. Flower is ruffled and the ruffled edge is dark burgundy-purple. Very beautiful and unique. Tetraploid.

'Changeling'. Photo by SALTER

'Chinese Cloisonne'. Photo by MUNSON

'Child of Fortune'–1987 (Elizabeth Hudson Salter). Semievergreen. 15 in. Midseason. A 3 in., pale pink flower, with an exquisite washed eye of chalky lavender and violet. The large eye is etched, by a tiny, magenta edge, and set off by a yellow-green throat. Diploid.

'Chinese Temple Flower'–1980 (Ida Munson). Evergreen. 24 in. Early midseason. An exceptional 5 in., flower blending lilac and lavender-blue, with a small, precise, dark royal-purple eye, topping the yellow-green throat. Special. Tetraploid.

'Child of Fortune'. Photo by SALTER

'Chinese Temple Flower'. Photo by MUNSON

'Dark Persuasion'–1987 (Elizabeth Hudson Salter). Semidormant. 20 in. Early. One of the season's first eyed cultivars to bloom, this 3¼ in., beautiful flower of lavender-purple, has a dark black-purple eye, and a yellow-green throat. Diploid.

'Dark Symmetry'–1987 (Elizabeth Hudson Salter). Semievergreen. 19 in. Midseason. A 3½ in., beautiful, dark purple bloom, with a lighter washed purple eye pattern, that is etched in darker purple, and punctuated by short, light lavender midribs in the eye pattern. Diploid.

'Chinese Cloisonne'–1984 (Ida Munson). Semievergreen. 28 in. Early to midseason. A 5 in., pastel cream-melon with an eye zone of palest blue-violet, edged in violet-plum. The petals overlay the sepals and are generally raised in the throat area, giving the impression of ruffles extending into the throat. Tetraploid.

'Dark Symmetry'. Photo by SALTER

'Designer Jeans'. Photo by SIKES

'Degas Ballet'–1987 (Stamile). Dormant. 28 in. Early midseason. A medium, 5¼ in., rick pink flower with a rose-red eye, and strong green throat. Form is round and flat, with deeply scalloped ruffling. Tetraploid.

'Designer Image'–1987 (Sikes). Dormant. 20 in. Midseason. A beautiful, very round, wide petaled, 6 in., ruffled lemon-beige, with a large, deep lavender eye zone, and deep lavender petal edges, and yellow-green throat. Tetraploid.

'Designer Rhythm'. Photo by SIKES

'Designer Image'. Photo by SIKES

'Designer Jeans'–1983 (Sikes). Dormant. 34 in. Midseason. A very large, 6½ in., cream-mauve-pink, with distinctively marked, deep lavender eye zone, and deep lavender petal edges. Yellow-green throat. Tetraploid.

'Designer Rhythm'–1987 (Sikes). Dormant. 25 in. Midseason. Ruffled, large, 6 in., light lavender-mauve blend, with large deep lavender eye zone, complemented by deep lavender petal edges and green yellow throat. Tetraploid.

'Duke of Durham'–1977 (Elliott). Dormant. 29 in. Midseason late. Large, 6 in., cooper-brown, with purple eye zone, and green throat. Diploid.

'Duke of Durham'. Photo by ELLIOTT

'Elizabeth Anne Hudson'–1975 (Munson). Evergreen. 26 in. Early midseason. Large, 5½ in., peach-pink, boldly edged and eyed in plum-purple. A classic. Tetraploid.

'Elizabeth Anne Hudson'. Photo by MUNSON

'Empress of Bagdad'–1987 (Munson). Evergreen. 28 in. Midseason to late. A 5½ in., large, broad, full, overlapped, ruffled, and fluted, ivory-peach tinted and toned in palest pink, ivory, buff, lilac and beige, with a large precise eye zone or petal spot of rose-beige. The throat is very round, small, yellow-green, with a green heart. Tetraploid.

'Enchanter's Spell'–1982 (Elizabeth Hudson Salter). Evergreen. 18 in. Midseason. This 3 in. flower of palest ivory, with a multilayered eye pattern, which starts out near the throat as a lavender wash, and ends on the petals with a finely etched, eye edge of dark purple. Throat is a bright yellow-green. Diploid.

'Enchanter's Spell'. Photo by SALTER

'Fairy Firecracker'–1984 (Elizabeth Hudson Salter). Evergreen. 15 in. Midseason. This round, full formed, 2¾ in., flower is a bright blending and fusing of deepest orange, coral, red and yellow. The colors meld to form a unique flower pattern which resembles an explosion of color. The intense color in the petals and sepals is set off by a large, patterned yellow throat with tiny, lime-green heart. Diploid.

'Fairy Firecracker'. Photo by SALTER

'Frandean'–1979 (Peck). Dormant. 20 in. Midseason late. The 6½ in., broad, full flowers are a delicate pristine lavender-pink-lilac, with a violet-lavender eye. The throat is small and yellow-green. A very feminine, beguiling and delicate cultivar. Tetraploid.

'Grand Wazir'–1978 (Cruse). Evergreen. 24 in. Early midseason. A broad, full, round, medium-large, 5 in., flower of russet-maroon, with a bold, black-red eye zone. Strong green throat. Special. Diploid.

'Gypsy Spell'–1975 (Cruse). Evergreen. 26 in. Early midseason. A medium-large, 5½ in., flower of clear buff-yellow, with a bold, electric-red eye, and a green throat. Special. Diploid.

'Jason Salter'–1987 (Elizabeth Hudson Salter). Evergreen. 18 in. Early midseason. A round, full formed, recurved, 2¾ in., corn-yellow flower, with a wide lavender-purple eye area, set above a lime-green throat. Lighter lavender midribs bisect the eye zone area on the petals forming a pattern. Diploid.

'Jason Slater'. Photo by SALTER

'Kenneth Cobb'. Photo by ELLIOTT

'Jim McGinnis'–1983 (Elizabeth Hudson Salter). Semievergreen. 14 in. Midseason. A beautiful, 2¾ in., flower of very pale peach-pink, with a bold, circular eye pattern, of intense rose-red. The eye dominates this tiny flower extending well into the contrasting petal color. A deep green throat, adds to its visual beauty. Diploid.

'Lady Violet Eyes'. Photo by SALTER

'Jim McGinnis'. Photo by SALTER

'Kenneth Cobb'–1986 (Elliott). Dormant. 22 in. Midseason. A cream-white, 6½in., full formed, recurved, flower with a pale rose halo, and large, bright green throat. Diploid.

'Lady Violet Eyes'–1986 (Elizabeth Hudson Salter). Semidormant. 18 in. Midseason. A beguiling, full formed, lightly ruffled, 3 in., flower of light lavender-purple, with a beautiful washed eye of blue-violet. The eye pattern is different and distinctive, with a yellow-green throat. Diploid.

'Lhasa'–1977 (Kirchhoff). Evergreen. 24 in. Extra early. Large, 6 in., lavender-purple blend, with purple eye zone, and large green throat. Diploid.

'Masque'–1977 (Crochett). Dormant. 22 in. Early. Very pretty, broad, full formed, medium, 5½ in., pale lavender-pink, with deeper lavender-purple eye, and green throat. Diploid.

'Panache'–1983 (Munson). Evergreen. 28 in. Midseason to late. An incredibly exciting, edged, 5 in., flower of warm flesh to salmon-pink, richly edged, and eyed in a dark plum-purple. The edge is wide, and prominent, and the eye bold, and dramatic. Tetraploid.

'**Pandora's Box**'–1980 (Talbott). Evergreen. 19 in. Early midseason. Small, 4 in., broad, full form, ruffled, cream, with a small, distinctive, purple eye, and yellow-green throat. Beguiling. Diploid.

'**Paper Butterfly**'–1983 (Morss). Semievergreen. 24 in. Early. A large, 6 in., cream-peach and blue-violet blend, with blue-violet eye zone, and green throat. Quite unique. Extraordinarily handsome. Tetraploid.

'Paper Butterfly'. Photo by MORSS

'**Persian Pixie**'–1985 (Elizabeth Hudson Salter). Evergreen. 16 in. Midseason. A bright blend of orange, peach, salmon and coral, with a paler, washed watermark, surrounding a bright yellow throat, and green heart. The 2½ in. flowers are very round, full, overlapped, and delicately ruffled. Diploid.

'Persian Pixie'. Photo by SALTER

'**Purple Storm**'–1985 (Webster). Dormant. 30 in. Midseason late. A very showy, 5½ in., purplish pink, with large, deep purple eye, the petals are edged in deep purple. Gold-green throat. Tetraploid.

'Purple Storm'. Photo by WEBSTER

'**Siloam Eye Shocker**'–1987 (R. Henry). Dormant. 17 in. Midseason. A very bold, lightly ruffled, 3½ in., light rose-red, with a very large, deeper rose-red eye zone, and green throat. Diploid.

'Siloam Eye Shocker'. Photo by HENRY

'**Siloam Heart Warmer**'–1987 (R. Henry). Dormant. 18 in. Midseason. Very unique, very ruffled, 4 in., light rose-red, with deeper red eye zone, and yellow-green throat. Diploid.

'Siloam Heart Warmer'. Photo by HENRY

'Siloam Night Ring'–1987 (R. Henry). Dormant. 18 in. Midseason. Very full, round formed, slightly recurved, 3¾ in., cream-pink, with black-burgundy eye zone, and small green throat. Diploid.

'Siloam Night Ring'. Photo by HENRY

'Sorcerer's Spell'–1985 (Elizabeth Hudson Salter). Semievergreen. 14 in. Midseason. A beguiling 3¼ in., flower of pale lavender-pink, with a large, bold, circular eye pattern, that extends halfway onto the petals. Flowers are very round, accentuating the eye pattern. Small green throat. Diploid.

'Sorcerer's Spell'. Photo by SALTER

'Tripoli'–1982 (Talbott). Evergreen. 28 in. Early midseason. A large, broad, flat lilac-pink, with bold eye of lavender-plum, and green throat. Excellent qualities and very special. Diploid.

'Violet Osborne'–1987 (Kirchhoff). Evergreen. 24 in. Early midseason. A classic double form, is this 5 in., peach, with orange-red eye zone, and green throat. Diploid.

'Violet Osborne'. Photo by KIRCHHOFF

'Windsor Watermark'–1982 (Munson). Evergreen. 26 in. Early midseason. An impressive, large, 6 in., flower of blue-violet-lavender, with a bold patterned or eye of chalky violet. Unique and low growning. Tetraploid.

'Witch Stitchery'–1986 (Morss). Semievergreen. 26 in. Extra early. A large 5½ in., cream, with lavender eye zone, edged purple, with green throat. Tetraploid.

'Witch Stitchery'. Photo by MORSS

'Witch's Thimble'–1981 (Elizabeth Hudson Salter). Evergreen. 18 in., Midseason to late. A 2½ in., enchanting, flower of palest lemon-cream, with a bright, bold eye, of black-purple, and yellow-green throat. Diploid.

'Wounded Heart'–1985 (Sikes). Evergreen. 26 in. Midseason. A 5½ in., light orange, heart-shaped bloom, with a dramatically marked eye zone area of scarlet that bleeds down into the small green throat, and out onto the petals. Very different. Tetraploid.

'Witch's Thimble'. Photo by SALTER

'Wounded Heart'. Photo by SIKES

3

Hybridizing

If one grows daylilies it is inevitable that one will sooner or later become intrigued with the idea of crossing them and creating new hybrids. Unlike many other genera the daylily is extremely easy to cross pollinate and the time and effort required to produce blooming size plants from seed is truly minimal.

Before embarking on a breeding program one should have the basic facts of the reproductive elements of the flower and the techniques of breeding well in mind. Simplisticly, as with most plants, pollen is placed on the end of the pistil which is called the stigma. The pistil is the long, thin, protruding, tubelike member or element in the center of the flower. The end of the pistil or stigma is hairy and sometimes sticky or moist to help receive and retain the pollen as it is past over the surface. The anthers, which contain the pollen, are carried at the ends of the stamens which surround the pistil and are attached at the throat of the flower. The pollen from one flower is crossed to the pistil (stigma) of another and the fertilization process begins. Three to four days after pollination the dead flower drops off, leaving the small round ovary that has been fertilized and begun to grow. The ovary will grow and develop into a large seed pod or capsule with 10–12 seed per pod. The pod range from about the size of a nickel to that of a quarter depending upon the flower type. The pod matures in 5–8 weeks depending on weather, climatic conditions, rainfall, etc. Crosses made in the late fall will mature faster than those made in the early spring or summer.

Seed should be collected as the capsule matures, drying and beginning to split at the end. Seed can be planted immediately or held for planting in the late fall or early spring, whichever is easiest within one's locality. If one is breeding a significant number of dormants, seed should be refrigerated for a period of 5–6 weeks prior to planting to help break dormancy and insure germination. This is not required if one decides to plant outside in the late fall just prior to the arrival of winter.

Breeding is rewarding! To see the fruits of ones efforts come to fruition is exciting. Most people just start crossing—asking themselves, "I wonder what would happen if I crossed plant A with plant B?"—then making the cross. But if one is serious about crossing the establishing of breeding lines is essential and just a bit more complicated.

It is my firm belief that anyone who crosses daylilies should define the objectives for which they are striving. Whether that is a simple goal such as "broad, round, ruffled pink daylilies," or a more comprehensive, complex program of "breeding miniature, red daylilies 10 in. tall, with flowers 1 in. and under, with green throats, and round, ruffled, forms, branched stems that carry 25 buds, etc."! This is an ideal objective since no daylily presently exists at that level of finish and quality—though perhaps some are close. Such an objective reguires a complex program and would take many years to achieve. No matter the degree of effort required to reach a goal it is best to know where one is trying to go! In other words one needs to know where one is going before purchasing a ticket!

Once a program is set one needs to acquire the best material available in order to realize the objectives of that program. Some new materials are very expensive and some can be difficult to use. And yet breeding is about producing significant plants in a short period of time and will take a lifetime to achieve. Consequently cultivars that clearly make quantum leaps ahead of the crowd are usually invaluable no matter what the cost since they allow the breeder to reduce the time line.

Breeding involves orchestrating many different characteristics and all at the same time. Most breeders can orchestrate the flowers, but have a difficult time working for all those other characteristics, like branching, vigor, erect scapes, sunfastness, ruffles, texture, eyes, edges, green throat, etc. which a fine cultivar requires. Generally one should start with parents that have the most desirable of those characteristics one is planning to improve. If one plans to breed round, ruffled, reds that are sunfast this may be as simple as breeding a low, round, ruffled, sunfast yellow to a strong, bright red. One cannot expect many low, round reds from the initial cross, but the best in the cross are then selected (those low, round, ruffled, red or reddish in color), and crossed together in an f2 program. Other options include back crossing to the red parent, or several out crosses to other red cultivars. The process is continued year after year as one begins to narrow the gap and the red color begins to be refined and intensified, and ruffling finally begins to emerge. Yet this is a never-ending process for one never reaches his goal or perfection! In reality one may reach the original goal set, but new goals—or adjusted goals—soon take the place of the original. Each year as one sees the progress and qualities achieved, one immediately longs for greater advances and so adjusts or modifies the goals.

It is essential that one not ignore any aspect of a plant, if one is to be successful. Poor characteristics will always emerge so one has to be aware of any "bad" characteristics in a plant—or line. Sooner or later they will emerge and very often in the cross that possesses all the other good characteristics sought. One can not escape the use of some plants with undesirable or poor traits, but one must manage these traits so as to minimize their impact.

Breeding does not require great effort but the recording of each cross, tagging the flowers crossed, collecting the seeds and recording the cross on the seed containers, making the garden tags that follow the cross until it blooms, sowing the seed, lining out the seedlings, studying and selecting the seedlings, numbering the seedlings to be kept, etc., does! It is all part of a regime that must be followed. However, for all the work there is nothing quite as uplifting and joyous as producing an incredibly beautiful, new cultivar—especially one that makes a quantum leap beyond its two parents, one which makes the heart stand still!

When this miracle happens one immediately begins to consider the commercial aspects of the cultivar. Normally one has to wait a couple of years while the testing and evaluation of the plant takes place. Its health, vitality, vigor, its ability to sustain, as well as its uniqueness in an already overblown commercial market must be studied and assessed. Once its quality is validated, one of the first steps should be to register the cultivar with the American Hemerocallis Society. Forms can be obtained from the Society's registrar. For a small fee together with the completed forms the cultivar can be registered with the Society, after which the name and all pertinent information is published by the Society in a checklist. With thousands of named cultivars presently registered with the A.H.S. finding a name that has not been used is difficult!

Every breeder hybridizing and growing daylilies has a special way to cross flowers, collect and hold seed for planting, as well as sow seed. Most of these individual approaches work rather well, so the breeder need only determine the approach best for him. I sow my seed in the early fall after they have been refrigerated for 4–5 weeks or longer. A flat is made up of a loose sandy loam—quite friable. The seed are sown in rows about 18 in. apart, about ⅓ in. deep, and about an ⅛ in. apart in the rows. The first seeds germinate in 10–14 days and are usually ready for transplanting in 6–8 weeks. A weekly application of liquid fertilizer is helpful in moving the transplanted plants ahead. In very mild climates 50–75% will bloom the first year. In more severe areas with cold winters and short growing seasons, seedlings can take up to three years to flower.

Once a special cultivar is developed the need to propogate it becomes a prime consideration. Daylilies are normally increased by plant division, with their multiplications being formed at the base of the plant where the foliage and the crown of the plant merge. The crown with its individual plants can be cut into sections and planted. An individual plant can produce a single increase or as many as 25—depending upon the culture and its natural characteristic ability to increase. Most cultivars can be forced to increase beyond their normal genetic state with special or extraordinary care, such as growing them in full sun in a rich organic soil and a carefully planned regime of water and fertilizer. Watering is done systematically so that the soil does not dry out. The fertilizer used is high in nitrogen and applications can occur as frequently as every several days. This approach is generally used by most breeders and growers of daylilies today.

Another method to increase plants is tissue culture, which has been recently applied to daylilies. With tissue culture millions of plants can be produced in a very short period of time from a very small number of plant divisions. Many plants are presently being propagated by this technique, especially by large wholesale nursery companies. As the demands for daylilies by the buying public increase, propagation by tissue culture will undoubtedly increase as well.

The process involves producing a tissue culture by isolating a plant cell and aseptically placing it into a vessel of nutriment medium under controlled enviromental conditions (quality and quantity of illumination, temperature, humidity, etc.), with the objective being to obtain rapid asexual multiplication of plant cells or plants. Any green tissue composed of cells with competent nuclei is a suitable subject for the initiation of a plant tissue culture. Vegetative shoot tips, terminal stem tips, axillary buds, stem sections, leaf sections, repoductive parts—such as microspores, megaspores, ovules, embryos, seeds and spores, as well as isolated cells and protoplants (wall-less cells)—are used in this process.

This process appears to have few problems. However, it has been noted that if a "tissue cultured" plant is reused for the tissue culture process there may be problems with mutations occuring, and that all plants developed may not be identical to the original cultivar. The process appears to be a very acceptable solution to produce hundreds of thousands of plants at a very reasonable cost and in a very compressed period of time.

The future is extremely bright for the daylily. Many options exist so one needs to select the characteristics for which one will breed as carefully as possible. Many promising new avenues require great effort and a multi-year commitment which challenges the best of us. Colors will continue to be refined, but most color breaks have already been established—with the exception of blue! I do not foresee dramatic color changes. However, the explosion of forms—doubles, spiders, miniatures, and flat, round, ruffled—will continue with major efforts being directed to doubles and spiders. Patterns, edges, and bold eyes will emerge strongly as breeding for them becomes easier. We should see red edges on pastel daylilies, white edges on red daylilies, gold and ivory edges, and "metallic" threads woven through out the ruffled "bubbly" edges of all colors. Strong green throats will become standard fare. Scapes must be worked on, as well as branching and vitality. The need to breed cultivars from which the spent flowers drop quickly from the scape will become increasingly important and a major concern as daylilies become increasingly more popular for landscape use—whether in parks, naturalized settings, country estates, home gardens or commerical landscapes. For all the progress that has been made over the past 50 years, the real challenge lies ahead as the future of daylilies is determined by today's breeders and those of the next decade or two.

4

Landscaping with Daylilies

The daylily has often been called the perennial supreme, and surely if there is such a one it is this incredible plant. It possesses great visual variety, beauty and stamina, adapting easily to the growing conditions in vast areas of the world, ranging from semitropical conditions to the cold and more rugged climates of such diverse regions as Europe, Asia, Australia and North and South America.

It is a unique plant in that it has both evergreen and deciduous (dormant) foliage types, and many subtle foliage variations between the two.

Many of the early daylily hybrids were tall, normally 36–48 in., suitable only for the standard perennial border and then generally being relegated to the back of the border.

Modern hybridizers have changed all that, so many of the most recent hybrids have become almost a bedding plant with low scapes that range from 12–18 in. tall. The gardener now has several options as to how the daylilies can be used. How each gardener decides to use this wide array now depends only on personal taste, other perennials the gardener wishes to use, and whether one is a gardener, collector, or daylily connoisseur!

The daylily generally has excellent foliage suitable for either mass plantings or featured specimens. While the foliage of the genus remains straplike, a wide variety of heights ranging from 12–48 in. on the taller growing varieties is now available. Further, foliage habit is now arching, fountaining and recurving or upright, pointed and spearlike, or variations of all of them. Foliage color is generally a "leaf" green, but leaf color varies from a chartreuse-lime to a dark blue-green. Generally plants are not classified by foliage type except as dormant, semidormant, semievergreen or evergreen.

The intense breeding over the past 15 years to reduce the height of daylily scapes has been successful and now allows the plant to be viewed differently and used in different ways, though largely as a modern bedding plant. The daylily is ideally suited for this kind of use and so makes a stunning planting.

One of the major difficulties a bedding plant of many colors has is that if the landscape is not well planned so as to use similar or harmonious color groupings, the bed tends to take on a crazy-quilt appearance. The quiet harmony a single color can bring to a planting is invaluable.

The daylily is ideally suited to be a major plant group in a perennial border, whether the border features low, medium and tall cultivars with a range of bloom seasons (early, midseason and late) exclusively, or as a companion to other perennials. The effectiveness of a mixed border of daylilies, iris, phlox, poppies and similar perennials has yet to be surpassed, though the overwhelming beauty of a border made up only of daylilies is difficult to improve upon.

Despite the intense recent breeding efforts to reduce daylily scape height, daylilies are still available in heights of 36–48 in., and these monarchs of the aristocratic garden can be most effectively used against a hedge, wall, fence or architectural element. The foliage on such cultivars is generally bold and dramatic. Once the plant has formed a clump the foliage is generally quite symmetrical and takes on the look of a shrub with fountaining foliage or soft, bayonetlike fronds. A particular cultivar can be featured as an individual sentinel or in a group like palace guards grouped to feature some special emissary, like a flowering shrub, Japanese Maple, Mugo Pine, a Chinese sculpture, or a Japanese lantern. The uses for daylilies are almost endless depending only upon the gardener's imagination, aesthetic taste and willingness to seek out the very best.

'Betty Warren Woods'–1987 (Munson) an excellent example of the new wider ruffling and crimped edges. All photos in this chapter by the author.

'Copper Dawn'–1988 (Munson) a very good example of the fuller and more voluptuous new form.

'Court Magician'–1988 (Munson) a super example of the delicately ruffled petals, full overlapped, round, form and large lighter eye.

'Dunedin'–1989 (Munson) a very good example of the broad, sculptured look with excellent ruffling.

Colors of daylilies range from near white through all shades of cream, lemon-yellow, gold and orange to apricot-coral, pink through salmon, flesh-pink, rose, to red, burgundy, black-red to purple, magenta, violet-plum, lavender and many gradations between. All the colors of the spectrum are represented save blue and absolute white. Flowers range in size from 1½ in. to 10 in., although a few are even smaller or larger. They appear in a wide array of forms from round to lily-shape, to flat and ruffled, to full and tailored to spider and trumpet-shape with again an endless array of variations in between. Daylilies are self-colored and eyed. Eyes may be small or narrow and band-like to large, bold and flashy. Eye colors are generally deeper and most are red, rose, rose-red, burgundy-wine or purple. Watermark eyes, generally lighter eye zones the

'Edessa'–1988 (Munson) an example of the crepe textured, broad petaled form with light fluting and ruffles.

'Emma Bovary'–1988 (Munson) a super example of the voluptuous recurving form, with a two tone halo and large throat.

'Grand Palais'–1987 (Munson) an example of the full, broad, flat and overlapped, round form. Slight ruffling and fluting and a very large lighter eyezone and large open throat.

'Lauriana'–1988 (Munson) an example of the new shade of lilac white.

same hue as the petal color, have emerged in the past 15 years. They are normally soft, subtle and add a "quiet" refinement and beauty to the overall bloom, much as a delicate tracery enhances the beauty of a cathedral "Rose Window". Petal stripes, a raised rib normally found in the middle of the flower petals, can be the color of the petal, a lighter shade, ivory, white, pink or lilac. The strong white mid-stripe has never been looked upon as a truly desirable characteristic in darker colors since the stripe does tend to add a fussiness or busyness to the overall flower that makes for a chaotic affect in the garden.

The throats of daylilies range from orange, gold, lemon-cream to green with green being the color preferred by most breeders and collectors today. The color of the throat can add immeasurably to the overall appeal of the flower. One day orange may also be viewed as a desirable color.

A new characteristic—ruffely, frilled, fringed and bubbly edges have emerged over the past 10 years. These edges are new and interest in them is growing so breeders are intensifying their efforts to make such types more readily available. Presently edges are mostly gold, dark purple or magenta-burgundy, and near white.

The palette of daylily material is broad, comprehensive, highly varied and in many cases exotic and esoteric. This enormous array of flower types only compounds the landscaping problem—never simplifies it. It is somehow more difficult to paint with 100 colors then it is with five because of the much larger number of choices to be made. The creator of a daylily garden may be overwhelmed by all the types, colors and heights to choose from. This diversity makes planning an absolutely essential first step.

Most growers, and collectors tend to want one of each of the daylilies seen thereby creating a hodgepodge of color and form and style. Such an approach makes for a tapestry of discord with the general effect created quite overwhelming and not necessarily "beautiful";—breathtaking but not "quiescent"; flamboyant but not one of quiet repose. Since most gardens tend to be a repository of collected plants, received as gifts or purchased on impulse and rarely planted for individual show or effect it is difficult to achieve a visual picture with style, harmony and visual joy.

To create an effective garden or series of garden pictures one must start with a plan that recognizes at least some of the following:

1. Location of existing trees.
2. Architectural elements such as walls, paths, drives, etc.
3. Prevailing sunlight, wind and annual rainfall.
4. Man-hours to maintain the desired effect of the garden.
5. Funds required to implement the most basic of plans.
6. Appropriate plants, i.e. materials adaptable to the environmental region in which the garden is located.

With these elements firmly in mind the gardener can begin to develop the geometrical shapes that will ultimately become the flower or plant beds of the garden. Once this is done the gardener must visualize in the "mind's eye" the images to be created. The more complicated the image the more difficult the design and the implementation. Once this is done a palette of plants must be chosen and with them the painting of the garden picture can begin.

In producing any garden one must be keenly aware that maintenance and "required care" are crucial ingredients to success. Many plants require major maintenance or constant "tender loving care," which can defeat a garden before it is started, so remember that no matter how pretty a plant, "pretty is as pretty does" and the daylily does very well, offering much beauty for a minimum of expense, time and care.

In planting daylilies the gardener must be keenly aware that these plants respond and grow toward the strongest light and therefore often face in a direction not compatible with the desired garden picture or image to be created! The daylily is a plant that enjoys full sun to part shade. If the garden is shady the directional light problem becomes more difficult to manage, so the garden view must be adjusted to such garden conditions.

A background hedge of ilex, viburnum, or other evergreen shrubs is very effective in controlling the view as well as directing the daylily bloom in the desired orientation.

Daylilies can rarely be used successfully under trees unless the trees are tall, creating a "dappled" high shade. The tree roots must not be invasive and overtake the bed before the picture can be completed.

Trees like magnolias, maples, sweetgum, etc., develop fiberous roots which tend to fill a bed within a few months. Oaks and pines are less of a problem, but if used the roots must be managed. The gardener must guard against having to replant a bed annually for most perennials require 2–3 years to become "established" and reach their full potential.

'Maison Carree'–1988 (Munson) an example of the very opulent, broad, overlapped form, delicate deep ruffles and flutes on the petal edges, and a small throat.

'Malaysian Monarch'–1986 (Munson) an excellent example of the round, bold, broad, recurved showy definitely voluptuous form, with a bold, large light round eye.

'Merry Witch'–1984 (Munson) example of the bold deep ruffled broad form.

'Moon Vespers'–1986 (Munson) a very good example of the broad, full, overlapped, ruffled and frilled voluptuous form. A very small throat.

Mulches tend to reduce garden maintenance and daylilies respond well to them. Mulches keep the ground cool and moist in summer, and warmer or more evenly constant in temperature in winter. However, guard against the soil becoming too dry under a mulch. If this happens it is difficult to wet the soil again, particularly without a good soaking rain. A mulch should be attractive (color and texture complementary to the picture to be produced), easily maintained, refurbished from time to time and not subject to packing or caking which tends to keep water away from the roots. Cypress bark, ground pine bark, oak leaves, pine needles, etc. are all effective mulches that last reasonably well, and each adds its own effective finishing touch to the visual nuances of the garden picture to be created.

'Panache'–1983 (Munson) a super example of a bold dark eye pattern and a dark small thread like edge on the recurved petals and sepals which are light ruffled.

'Prince of Venice'–1983 (Munson) an example of a broad, overlapped, flat, full form, with light fluting and ruffled, and a super three tone triangular eye pattern. Lighter splotches on the sepals and the throat area.

'Respighi'–1986 (Munson) an excellent example of a bold, round lightly recurved form, with a super bold lighter eye pattern.

'Semiramide'–1984 (Munson) example of the bold, round, full form, with an excellent eye pattern.

A garden should be a reflection of its owner or creator. Whether that garden is formal or informal, elegant or casual, large or small does not matter. But it should include daylilies in some way—that way only being limited by the creator's imagination or desires.

Because of the hybridizing revolution and its success in transporting the daylily to new heights of beauty and into the formal more intimate garden one tends to forget some of its earlier uses, i.e. woodland settings and naturalized plantings. With all of its modern panache and verve it is understandable that gardeners tend to forget the earlier uses of the plant. This is a serious shortcoming for daylilies still excel in natural woodland settings—being used magnificently in drifts along rivers, streams, in woodland glades, along drives, roads or meadow edges.

The landscape use of daylilies as a containerized plant on patios, balconies, etc. is only just emerging. The daylily is well adapted to being grown in pots or large containers. The lower scaped, more fashionable cultivars tend to adapt better and look better in containers than do the taller growing cultivars. The placement of daylilies on the patio, terrace or deck in containers is catching on and bringing a bit of spice to an otherwise cold architectural element.

The following illustrations are included to demonstrate several kinds of plantings in which daylilies can be successfully used. I hope they will stimulate the gardener's own imagination and enable him to create his own "garden picture"!

'Shisheido'–1988 (Munson) an example of the full, overlapped broad, voluptuous recurved form. Ruffled and frilled petal edges and very small throat.

Daylilies in South Carolina. Garden owner unknown. Photograph courtesy American Hemerocallis Society, Garden Slide.

Windmill Gardens. Sarah Sikes, Luverne, Alabama. Photograph by Ahston Johnson, American Hemerocallis Society, Garden Slide.

San Diego Wild Animal Garden. San Diego, California. Photograph courtesy American Hemerocallis Society, Garden Slide.

Court Yard of Ra Hansen, Winter Springs, Florida. Photograph by Jim April, American Hemerocallis Society, Garden Slide.

Paradise Lane at Wimberlyway Gardens, Gainesville, Florida. Photograph by R. W. Munson, Jr.

Fairy Firefly at Wimberlyway Gardens, Gainesville, Florida. Photograph by Elizabeth Hudson Salter.

Iron Gate Gardens. Van M. Sellers. Kings Mountain, North Carolina. Photograph by Love Seawright, American Hemerocallis Society, Garden Slide.

Garden of Ra Hansen. Winter Springs, Florida. Photograph by Jim April, American Hemerocallis Society, Garden Slide.

Windmill Gardens. Sarah Sikes, Luverne, Alabama. Photograph by Sarah Sikes, American Hemerocallis Society, Garden Slide.

Daylily World. David Kirchhoff, Sanford, Florida. Photograph by David Kirchhoff.

Daylily World. David Kirchhoff, Sanford, Florida. Photograph by David Kirchhoff.

Daylily World. David Kirchhoff, Sanford, Florida. Photograph by David Kirchhoff.

Garden of Howard Hite. Pontiac, Michigan. Photograph by Howard Hite, American Hemerocallis Society, Garden Slide.

Garden of Alex Goldberg. Glen Cove, Long Island, New York. Photograph courtesy American Hemerocallis Society, Garden Slide.

Garden of the late Lucille Williamson. Jasper, Texas. Photograph courtesy American Hemerocallis Society, Garden Slide.

Big Tree Daylily Garden. Merle Kent, Longwood, Florida. Photograph by Jim April, American Hemerocallis Society, Garden Slide.

Big Tree Daylily Garden. Merle Kent, Longwood, Florida. Photograph by Jim April, American Hemerocallis Society, Garden Slide.

Wimberlyway Gardens. Ida and Bill Munson, Gainesville, Florida. Photograph by Betty Hudson.

Wimberlyway
Gardens. Ida and Bill
Munson, Gainesville,
Florida. Photographs
by Betty Hudson.

Wimberlyway
Gardens. Ida and Bill
Munson, Gainesville,
Florida. Photographs
by Betty Hudson.

5

Horticultural Requirements

The daylily is a herbaceous perennial—a perennial that does not develop persistent woody tissue but dies down at the end of the growing season. It multiplies at the crown where a second plant emerges when it flowers or when off-shoots form at the base— ultimately forming a clump of ramets or divisions. The increase in the number of ramets varies depending upon the vigor of the individual cultivar and can be as few as one to as many as 15 annually. The amount of increase will govern the frequency with which a grower should propagate (divide) the clumps. If clumps become too large and too crowded quality of the bloom can be greatly reduced. In a well-cared-for garden with heavy, loam soil clumps can produce adequately for many years. In more sandy locations clumps should be divided every two to three years, to sustain bloom quality and plant vigor.

Propagation (or the dividing of clumps) is normally done in the fall or spring depending upon climate and geographical area. The clump to be propagated is dug and any excess soil shaken from its roots. The clump can then be washed so division lines are more easily seen, though this is not essential. Individual divisions (ramets) should be made if the cultivar is rare and the gardener wishes to increase the number of plants as quickly as possible. However, if the gardener wants a more established look in a planting immediately, the plants should be divided to include two or three divisions (ramets). The tops (foilage) are then trimmed and any excessively long roots are pruned back to about 6–8 in. from the base of the crown.

Once the clumps or plants have been dug and all excess soil removed or the plants washed dividing can begin. Excessive foliage should be removed, and I cut back the foliage of the clump to a height of 8–10 in. An assessment of the clump can now be made concerning how it should be divided. If the clump is quite mature the individual divisions may be pulled apart by hand. If on the other hand the crown is still solid a knife is required for dividing. Holding the clump (plants) firmly, take a large (10–12 in.) knife and place it carefully between two divisions with the cutting edge along the top of the crown. Cut straight down and divide the clump in half. Continue this process until the clump is divided into as many smaller units as it can safely be divided. If there are 8–10 divisions in the clump, four or five seperate plants can probably be produced. Care must be taken when cutting that a reasonable number of roots remain attached to the crown to enable the plant to sustain itself while other roots are being produced.

The divided plants are now ready for replanting. If the crown has been severely cut it is wise to dust the cut with a standard fungicide to protect against possible rot, particularly if the weather is extremely hot and humid. Once treated the daylily can then be planted. The hole should be dug sufficiently large so that the roots can be placed in it without having to be twisted. The crown should be covered with ¾–1½ in. of soil. If the plant is planted too deeply it will generally sit and sulk taking weeks to recover, so too-shallow planting is "better" than too-deep. The loose soil should be worked in around the roots filling in the hole. Tamp the soil firmly around the roots and water. The plant, if healthy, will begin to grow almost immediately. It is best to keep the planting on the dry side rather than too wet during this period of adjustment.

PROPAGATION

(Illustrations courtesy of Harold H. Kirk, Concord, N.C.)

Freshly dug unwashed daylily clump.

Daylily clump with foliage and scapes cut back to 6–8 in.

Washing off excess soil from daylily clump for easier division.

Daylily clump with knife positioned to make first dividing cut.

Daylily clump divided in half showing exposed crown area.

Single divided daylily plant set in prepared garden bed ready for soil to cover the roots.

Single daylily plant set and planted.

Tamping of soil around newly set daylily plant.

Planted daylily tamped, labeled and ready for watering.

114

The daylily has few maladies and is one of the easiest of all perennials to grow and maintain. But some basic rules should be followed to guarantee success. I will touch on them as well as try to bring into focus some potentially dangerous future problems.

The daylily will withstand much abuse, neglect and lack of attention by a gardener since it is not terribly demanding either of soil types or various soil "ph" counts and will generally sustain itself through major droughts or prolonged periods of rain, conditions that often destroy other, less stalwart perennials. This hardy constitution is (has been) both a blessing and a curse; an asset and a liability! People typically tend to do only that which is "essential" for a plant's survival. Survival for the daylily is no problem since the genus virtually thrives on neglect. But it does reward the simplest acts of horticultural consideration and can be transformed by a few, simple cultural practices normally involving only water, fertilizer and appropriate sunlight.

Where to plant the daylily is a major consideration, for if the location is poor no matter how much fertilizer or water is used the planting will always be substandard. The daylily should be planted in full sun to partial shade, but should receive at least 50% sun for best growing effects. The plant may grow adequately in heavy shade, but the plants will not grow as vigorously and scapes will be taller by 6–12 in. with bud count and branching greatly reduced. Morning sun through early afternoon is ideal.

The daylily will survive in very heavy, claylike soils or very fine, sandy soils, but will benefit greatly from the addition of sand and humus in heavy clay soils and humus and clay loam in sandy soils. A very friable loose loam soil is ideal. The soil does not have to be especially rich—a good average garden loam is actually best! This should be supplemented with several applications of a good, well-balanced fertilizer semi-annually. Soil should be reasonably porous so that water does not stand for prolonged periods of time. Daylilies tend to grow easily and multiply well (if given reasonable sun and a modicum of care) and should not be planted more closely than 20–30 in. on center if they are to remain undisturbed for at least 3–4 years. It should be pointed out that daylilies planted in very sandy soils will have a difficult time sustaining clump strength and producing quality blooms after the second year. Frequent propagation may be required.

As previously noted daylilies do not require heavy fertilization, but do respond superbly to an appropriate regime of watering. When temperatures are high a minimum of a weekly irrigation is desirable. During bloom season this should be increased to twice weekly with ½–1 in. of water being applied to beds during each irrigation period. In clay soils or more northerly latitudes they should be irrigated about five or six times a month during the hottest part of the summer. Appropriate mulches will reduce the need for water if care is taken to prevent the soil below the mulch from becoming severely dried out. In periods of extreme drought extraordinary care must be taken if the quality of the flowers is to be maintained. This could mean irrigating every other day if water rationing is not a problem.

Fortunately the daylily is bothered by few insects or pests, though more insects attack daylilies today than they did 30 years ago. However, their relative resistance to insects and disease helps make the daylily one of the most dependable perennials, yielding a satisfactory display each year with a minimum of dusting or spraying. Even so, growers should be on the alert for the appearance of a few pests. If and when insect damage does occur the following information may assist in identifying the pest which will in turn help in selecting the appropriate control measures. It must be pointed out here that I do not spray the garden of Wimberlyway with any insecticide or fungicide, and have not done so for over 15 years. I will not pretend that we do not have some insect damage but I've noticed we have no more than many other gardens, which maintain a regular regimen of corrective spraying. Our garden is large, sprawling over 13 acres. We apparently have established a micro-enviroment that allows for a reasonable balance with nature. Gardens of a smaller area or those within the city may reguire control measures simply because of the practices of adjacent gardeners.

115

Some of the more persistent pests that bother daylilies are:

SLUGS and SNAILS. Slugs and snails damage the tender young growth of daylilies particularly in the early spring along both coasts. They make ragged notches along the edges of leaves and sometimes holes in the middle. Their presence is normally marked by shiny, slime tracks left as the creatures crawl over the plants. If badly infested the slugs and snails may attack buds and flowers damaging petals and sepals. While rare, I have seen such severe infestations and can advise that they are difficult to bring under control.

Slugs and snails feed at night and generally hide by day in damp cool places, such as under leaves, stones, mulches, trash, soil, etc. Coarse, loose mulches around the daylilies or masses of dried, old, daylily leaves at the base of the plant provide favorable hiding places for the creatures. An annual clean up of hiding places will reduce the likelihood of damage.

APHIDS. Aphid damage on daylilies was first reported in California in 1954 by Quinn Buck. The aphid specie was later identified as *Myzus hemerocallis* Tak known previously only in China, Formosa and India. Infested plants are delayed in starting growth in the spring, and the new foliage is yellowed giving the appearance of a nitrogen deficiency. Feeding on the bloom buds causes warty protuberances and malformed flowers. Some flowers show severe discoloration as the flower segments open.

Various aphids have been identified, each having varying effects on daylilies. However the green peach aphid, *Myzus persicea,* which occasionally occurs on foliage of daylilies apparently has caused no visual damage.

THRIPS. At least five species of thrips have been found on daylilies. The most serious form of injury, shriveling and death of inflorescence while still undeveloped, is associated with thrips feeding on tender branches and flower buds. Flower stems may become bent and twisted. The feeding areas are rough and brown with several layers of corky, dead cells. Few or no flowers develop on heavily infested plants. Thrip *Frankliniella hemerocallis* can cause serious russeting of stems and distortion and loss of flowers. This thrip has been identified from New York to Wisconsin and Maryland to Florida.

SPIDER MITES. The two-spotted spider mite (Tetranychus urticae) and related species are present on ornamentals, vegetables, weeds, etc. in almost every garden. Mites feed by piercing the leaves, and injury on daylily foliage consists of speckled yellowish spots and sometimes reddish or brown areas. Heavily infested plants are stunted as the foliage declines and may be covered with fine webbing. Two-spotted spider mites are less than 1/50 in. long, yellowish green with two dark spots on the back. The *Cinna barinus* mite (found primarily in the southern states) is similar in size and possesses two brown spots although the general color of the adult female is brick-red or carmine. Spider mites increase rapidly during hot dry weather. One female may lay 100–200 eggs and a generation may be completed in five days. Spider mites live over the winter on various plants that retain their green leaves. Cleaning out cultivars to remove over-wintering hosts (such as chickweed) before spring growth starts is important in their control.

In this discussion the reader will note that I have not suggested that growers spray their daylilies! Consequently, I have not suggested any sprays or insecticides that could be used on slugs, thrips, aphids or spider mites. It seems there are more than sufficient sprays available in most garden centers to meet the needs of any grower of daylilies should they be so inclined. What I hope I have done is to make the gardener aware of the insects that do affect daylilies so he can be on the alert and take whatever action he deems appropriate. To spray or not to spray is a very complex matter and one that will not soon be resolved.

There are a few other maladies that must be mentioned to apprise the grower of potential problems he might encounter. Propagation of daylilies is generally done in the early fall (mid-August through September). Recently a problem known as "crown rot" has emerged in the South. Beginning some 15 or so years ago it was noticed that if given the right conditions—generally rain, moisture, heat, high humidity and an appropriately rich soil—a high percentage of certain cultivars developed crown rot. However, by delaying propagation 45–60 days or more it was noticed that the percentage of plants lost was greatly reduced, if not eliminated altogether. This is still a problem and not yet identified as related to any particular cultivar or strain of daylilies, but studies and assessments are underway. At present there does not seem to be a cure so I suspect a genetic or hereditary problem that is compounded when certain climatic conditions occur or come together. It is too early to assess this problem, but breeders of daylilies during the next 25 years will be facing a potentially dangerous situation—one that if not checked and controlled will certainly impact the future of daylilies.

A related condition in which an apparently healthy clump of 4–5 divisions is suddenly hit by crown rot for no apparent reason is also occurring. Such plants have been left undisturbed but simply begin to rot, starting with a single leaf which turns yellow, after which in a period of 4–5 days the entire clump has completely disintegrated. Obviously the rot began well before the telltale yellow leaf streak appeared, and by the time it does very little can be done to save the plant.

A third condition that has appeared in some isolated situations throughout the Midwest is called "the yellows". A clump develops a yellow streak in its foliage and the top begins to die back. Unlike a rotting plant, plants so stricken will ultimately recover but will probably not bloom in the year affected. The affected plant should be dug immediately, treated with a fungicide and replanted. This condition rarely occurs in the South and West, but has developed randomly and to varying degrees in the very rich, black soils of the Midwest. There does not seem to be any relation between a specific cultivar and the disease; the condition appears to be completely random.

These liabilities are listed only to inform. The gardener will rarely encounter them or at least not in any significant way. And yet, they can become serious problems for the grower and breeder of the future, so they must recognize that just because we have a basically trouble-free plant today it may not always be that way. We must protect our plant's heritage while expanding its horizons. Perhaps the greatest danger associated with the large number of people breeding daylilies (and basically for beauty alone), is that many cultivars will lose the vigor, stamina and hardy qualities that have allowed this magnificent perennial to survive through the ages.

EVERGREEN versus DORMANT. The daylily's unique characteristic of having both dormant and evergreen cultivars has set the stage for the broadest possible geographical adaptability and use of any perennial grown today. This characteristic also raises the interesting question of which foliage type is best suited for which geographical locations. Only one of the species has been identified as evergreen, *H. aurantiaca*. All the others are classified as dormant.

Through the breeders' art thousands of cultivars have emerged. These various cultivars are called "hard" evergreen, evergreen but hardy; "soft" evergreen, evergreen but tender; "hard" dormant, dormant but requiring a long dormant period; "soft" dormant, dormant but requiring only about a month or less of rest before starting into growth again; as well as semievergreen, semidormant with many gradations in between! It is difficult today to sort out these subtle variations and differences since there are now so many various gradations of foliage type. Thus many cultivars registered as dormant in colder regions are proving to be evergreen or semievergreen in semi- or subtropical regions. This interbreeding of foliage types is becoming so common that it is becoming increasingly difficult to accurately characterize plant foliage type. The so-called tender (soft) evergreen designation is still used today but it is not employed to the extent or the degree that it was 25 years ago.

With breeders in New England and the Midwest breeding evergreens to dormants and to evergreens the really tender ones are many times removed. With breeders in southern California, Texas, Louisiana and Florida breeding dormants to evergreens and dormants to dormants, a group of semievergreen plants with greater adaptability in more geographical sections is emerging. Adaptability will improve as we search for the *All American Daylily* that will grow everywhere! It is doubtful, however, that a cultivar ultimately happy in Canada will ultimately be happy in Florida—and vice versa. We have gone a long way to break down the barriers of evergreen versus dormant but there is still much that can be done. One must encourage the interbreeding of foliage types and discourage the breeding of similar foliage types, which may tend to restrict geographical adaptability. Growers are urged to explore the growing of cultivars from other geographic regions in an effort to learn more about what is truly hardy and adaptable (and to what extent) and what is truly tender and not adaptable (and to what extent) in their own area or garden microcosm.

A new grower should not attempt to build a daylily garden predicated only on a vast number of cultivars from a distant geographical location. But he should be willing to explore and test a few new daylilies from climates unlike his own. Growing daylilies in the climatic extremes (both heat and cold) can be a major challenge! But few genera adapt to so many different geographical locations and so many climatic conditions as well as the daylily. It is a wonder to be protected, preserved and expanded.

6

Judging the Daylily

Rules and regulations concering daylilies have been developed by the American Hemerocallis Society. Perhaps it is appropriate to briefly discuss its beginning.

The American Hemerocallis Society was founded in mid-July 1946 in Iowa and can be attributed largely to the dedication and love of hemerocallis by Helen Field Fischer of Shenandoah, Iowa. She had a local radio program on gardening and had quite a following for that time. She grew many kinds of flowers, but was especially attracted to daylilies and what they had to offer the gardener. She helped found the society and was assisted by her sister Jessey Shambaugh; daughter Gretchen Harshbarger; George Lennington of Kansas City, Missouri; Peter Sass and Henry Sass, growers and breeders of daylilies near Omaha, Nebraska; and many others from the area.

Round robin groups also participated. Some of these were sponsored by Helen Field Fischer's radio program, while others had been organized by *Flower Grower Magazine.* Everyone was to come and bring flowers for a show. Important people from the world of horticulture and hemerocallis were there. During the day it was decided to organize a society; it was named The Midwest Hemerocallis Society. With the phenomenal interest that soon evolved with people all over the United States wanting to participate, the name was changed to The Hemerocallis Society in 1949. In a historic meeting in Baton Rouge, Louisiana, in 1955, it became The American Hemerocallis Society. A modest beginning for a plant society that some 40 years later has a membership exceeding 4,000 and has members throughout the world. Besides the United States some of the other countries are: Argentina, Australia, Austria, Belgium, Canada, Czechoslovakia, Denmark, England, France, Guatemala, Iceland, Indonesia, Japan, Mexico, The Netherlands, New Zeland, Poland, Republic of South Africa, South Korea, Spain, Switzerland, U.S.S.R., West Germany, and Zimbabwe. From a very small but auspicious beginning has emerged one of the most dynamic and active plant societies in the world today. But because the future of the plant it represents is so incredible the society is bound to grow exceedingly fast and should have a membership of 25,000 within a very short time.

Judging and evaluation of daylilies is not an easy task and yet it is of major importance. Judging in my view is an assessment based upon precise rules, careful reason and personal experience. It is greatly governed by the judge's perception of quality and value. It is difficult to understand why one judge has a better grasp of these qualities than another, but it is clear the more extensive and more refined these experiences and perceptions are the better the judge and the judging. I have used the following analogy to relate judges to their experience and perception. If a judge had only crossed the desert on foot, a covered wagon might seem like a wonderful conveyance. If on the other hand he had previously traveled in a landrover, then the covered wagon would not be too impressive. If he had, however, experienced the elegance of a Rolls Royce

Silver Shadow, he could be thoroughly spoiled and even jaded in his preception of more typical transportation. Our perception closely relates to our experience!

Regrettably judging is not easy, and it is not always done well even by the trained and supposedly well-informed. The American Hemerocallis Society has established a group of National Awards and at the same time has adopted a series of rules and regulations governing the "how to" of judging. Information on these awards and judging is included in this chapter. But before we look at the "how to" we need to discuss some other problems.

Part of the problem with judging is that absolute, hard-and-fast rules that cannot be adjusted or modified over time—as time and experience change one's and society's preceptions—should not be set too firmly in place. The question then arises, and it is one that is hard to answer: When is the right time to review and modify the rule? And who decides?

Two words with which judges must constantly deal are "distinction" and "beauty" These two words are perfectly clear and yet deceptively ambiguous in meaning for most of us! Webster states, "distinction—indicates that something is distinguished by the mind or eye as being apart from or different from others; unique—beauty—the quality or aggregate of qualities in a person or thing that gives pleasure to the senses or pleasurably exalts the mind or spirit."

Round, flat and ruffled daylilies rarely appeared before 1950. Consequently, any such cultivar was automatically distinctive! Spidery or narrow petaled cultivars were the norm. Thirty-five years later narrow may be more distinctive than round if "uniqueness" is the yardstick of measure. I doubt that it is, but then who is to say?

One of the most difficult assessments to make these days is at what scape height is flower size in harmony with the plant? Most judges today feel that a small flower or miniature should not be associated with a tall scape and in fact mark such a cultivar down for a lack of balance or harmony. I totally disagree with this rather narrow perspective. In my view the key to balance is not flower size, but flower number and placement. Fifty or 60 buds form a bouquet and can be a marvelous vision, while a tall scape with 10–12 buds is not unlike an opera diva singing an aria while standing on stilts. The key is the total effect of the picture displayed.

At a recent Judges Seminar, a judge faulted an "S"-shaped scape remarking that it was not "straight"! I was bewildered. The stem was erect, ridged, well-branched and the "S" shape allowed the branching to be less crowded and more pleasing. All the scapes were the same size and shape. The judge, however, would not be swayed! A scape had to be more than "erect"—it had to be straight! An absolute! It seems to me judging must allow for a degree of reason to prevail all else being equal. Dogma is not acceptable even in the esoteric world of daylily judges and judging.

The present system is, of course, not perfect and regrettably poor judgments will be made from time to time. But the system is not altogether bad and it does give us a good foundation for making reasoned judgments and reasonable decisions about the quality of daylilies. There may be a time in the future when we and our daylilies have grown and prospered to a point where new, more elaborate rules and regulations will have to be promulgated, but for now what we have will do and do rather nicely—if only reasonable application of the rules can be achieved.

The American Hemerocallis Society recognizes two distinct categories of judges:

Exhibition Judges, who are schooled and trained in the art of judging at a hemerocallis show or exhibition.

Awards and Honors Judges (also referred to as "Garden Judges," revised 1987, Judges handbook), whose assessments authorize the yearly AHS Awards.

For specific details concerning judging, judging ethics and procedures, the reader is referred to the 1987, second revision, of the American Hemerocallis Society Handbook, *Daylily Judges Handbook,* Award and Honors Judges, Exhibition Judges. The Judges' Handbook reflects the latest recommendations of the American Hemerocallis

Society members, the Board of Directors, and the suggestions, outlined as guides, will lead to the upgrading of the daylily in the garden and in exhibition.

Therefore, I have included excerpts from the *Handbook,* since I feel that the accepted "yardstick" for measuring or evaluating a cultivar either in the garden or show should be known to all who grow and admire daylilies.

Judging Hemerocallis in the Garden

The Awards and Honors judge must be critical and objective in his thinking when voting. Cultivars must be evaluated by observing their performance as a complete plant in a garden. Judging should not be done on the performance of a flower alone. Plants should be seen as often as possible during the day, under varied conditions throughout the blooming season, and in as many gardens as possible. To assist in performing this duty, a set of good qualities has been developed to use as a guide. Therefore, in the evaluation process, each item in the Scale of Points should be carefully considered and applied. They are basic essentials for judging daylilies in the garden.

Awards and Honors Scale of Points
Judging Cultivar in Garden

FLOWER	45
Substance	5
Weather and temperature resistance	5
Clean, clear color	10
Form and size	10
Distinction	15
SCAPE	25
Strength in relation to flower(s)	10
Branching	5
Bud count	5
Height	5
FOLIAGE	
Clean, healthy, appealing in proportion to rest of plant	10
COMPLETE PLANT	
Pleasing plant proportions	20
TOTAL POINTS	100

1. The flower should always have good substance and texture and be resistant to all types of weather conditions.

Color is one of the most important factors in any garden. The flower must have clear, bright, clean color showing some luster or sheen to add to its beauty. If a blended color, all should be harmonious and pleasing. Many flowers improve in color by the end of the day, and this color change can give distinction. Some flowers fade, and this can add beauty.

Form and size of flowers should be consistent and typical of the cultivar. When size, form, and/or color pattern are the distinguishing factors, the bloom must be distinctive and noticeably different from the others on the market.

2. The scape should be graceful, erect, and have sufficient height and strength for the size of the flower and amount of branching. Branching well placed and spaced is a much desired quality, which should produce high bud count and good placement of buds and flowers.

3. Foliage should be healthy and attractive. Foliage free from disease is a prime consideration. There can be wide variations in color of leaves all adding to garden interest. Clumps with leaves that yellow too quickly are not desirable. Leaves should always be in proportion to the height of the scape and the size of the flower so that the complete plant is one of beauty.

4. Registered cultivars must be judged for what they are worth, but with seedlings, the judge always looks for the special quality defined as distinction. Too frequently clumps are so close together it is difficult to see the full potential of a daylily. No judge should vote for any cultivar which does not come up to the requirements necessary for a good garden daylily. Other desirable qualities may be looked for and considered, but the above basic qualities are essential.

Judging Hemerocallis in Exhibitions

NAMED CULTIVARS

When evaluating named cultivars of Hemerocallis, standards have been established by their hybridizers who registered each cultivar and described its particular characteristics. When a named cultivar is shown and displays its "approach" to perfection, it is referred to as being "true to cultivar".

When a named cultivar does not meet the hybridizer's standard, as registered, we begin a critical evaluation and deduct points as it deviates from the standard already established.

When it is determined that the quality being judged is true to cultivar, full credit is given. When it is determined that the quality being judged is not true to cultivar, the number of points deducted is determined by the severity and number of its faults.

Scale of Points for Named Cultivars

FLOWER	50
Color	10
Form	10
Texture	10
Substance	10
Size as to cultivar	10
SCAPE	35
Harmonious relationship to flower, height and strength	15
Buds	10
Branching	10
CONDITION AND GROOMING	15
TOTAL POINTS	100

FLOWER...... 50 points
Color—10 points
Color is evaluated by the visual sense of the quality of light which is reflected or transmitted by the flower. Color may be expressed in terms of three factors: hue (name of the color), chroma (purity or saturation) and brightness (value). Therefore, color has strong emotional appeal. While color can be enjoyed for its natural beauty without need for reason, an exhibition judge must determine if the color of the particular cultivar being judge is true to cultivar.

Merits—"True to cultivar" means the color is consistent with other specimens in the area in which the cultivar is grown.

Faults—The specimen is not true to cultivar (or not typical) because it is murky, dingy, streaked, dull, or has irregularity of marking.

Form—10 points
Form is the placement of petals and sepals in relation to each other, the definite shape of the flower. Petals may be curled, fluted, ruffled or tailored. Weather conditions influence form. A broken segment (petal or sepal) influences form but should be considered only under condition and grooming.

Merits—True to, or typical of cultivar.

Faults—Not true to cultivar, caused by malformation or uneven spacing of petals or sepals. If a bloom has serious faults or form, or presents spacing problems (crowding), it may be better to remove it before entering the scape.

Texture—10 points

Texture is the surface quality of the tissue structure, the smoothness or the roughness. Texture should enhance the color. Rough textures absorb light by adding richness through the shadows they cast in the dark colors. Smooth textures tend to reflect light, thereby making colors sparkle and glow, adding vividness.

Merits—True to, or typical of cultivar.

Faults—Not true to cultivar because it may be dull, lifeless, coarse, slick, unevenly ribbed or lacks luster.

Substance—10 points

Substance is the thickness of the tissue structure, the holding quality. In judging substance, the firmness and fineness as well as evenness of petals and sepals are points to consider. The amount of matter and moisture in the petals keeps them firm and crisp. These characteristics enable the flower to withstand weather conditions, retain form and freshness, and give life to the color. Cultural practices, both good and bad, with reference to soil preparation, watering, fertilization, protection from insects and disease, are reflected in substance. Substance with great durability may vary from thin and veil-like, with lacelike daintiness, to thick, crisp, fleshy substance.

Merits—True to, or typical of cultivar.

Faults—Not true to cultivar because tissue is thinning wilting, browning or melting, or it is limp.

Size—10 points

Both weather and geographical location influence size. Garden practices also influence size. When an exhibit is larger or smaller than it is registered it should be penalized.

Merits—True, or typical, or characteristic of cultivar.

Faults—Not true to cultivar because it is much smaller or larger than registered.

SCAPE. . . . . 35 points

Harmonious relationship to flower, height and strength—15 points. Height of scape should not exceed 36 in. as a general rule. However, to maintain an overall viewing appearance of the show, the show committee may have elected to limit the height of scapes. The relationship of branching, bud count, and size of flower of each cultivar is important in determining if exhibit is too short or too tall. Strength of scape is directly influenced by weather in that cool weather or excessive rain may cause abnormal crooks in a scape which may, or may not, detract from overall beauty of exhibit.

Merits—Typical, or true to cultivar; sturdy, supports inflorescence.

Faults—Not typical or true to cultivar because exhibit is too short or too tall; weak, limp, crooked, gross, fasciated (two or more scapes fused together and growing as one).

Buds—10 points

Do not expect a cultivar to do what it cannot do. If the Exhibition Judge does not know the cultivar, defer to the judgment of the other judges who do know the cultivar. If none of the judges on the panel knows the cultivar, exercise caution and discretion, especially when judging bud count of older cultivars.

Merits—True or typical of cultivar.

Faults—Not typical of cultivar because of too few, too scant or too crowded buds (meaning that the buds will not let the flowers open to their best advantage).

Branching—10 points

The caution mentioned under buds applies to branching. Branching may vary from one area of the country to another so use typical branching for the area in which the exhibits are grown as the standard.

Merits—Typical or true to cultivar.

Faults—Not typical in that the branching is crowded, scant, or totally inade-
quate for the cultivar.

CONDITION AND GROOMING .... 15 points
   Condition is determined by culture and is the actual physical state of the
specimen at the time of judging. Grooming is preparing the specimen for exhibit so
that it presents a clean and appealing appearance at the time of judging. Condition
and grooming include the merits or faults incurred in growing, spraying,
grooming, transporting to the show, and even accidents incurred in placement. If
the overall perfection of the flower has been altered more than 15 points, it will
then have to be reflected in the area of judging which is most adversely influenced,
i.e., form, color, substance, etc. On multiple bloom scapes the exhibitor should
remove faulty blooms. Seed pods and blasted buds should be removed. Dry, brown
tips on bracts should be trimmed to give a fresh appearance. Select only worthy
specimens for exhibition.
   Merits—Fresh, clean, well-groomed.
   Faults—Insect damage, seed pods left on, presence of insects, spent or faded
      flowers left on, spray residue, dust, dirt, pollen on segments, brown on
      bracts, proliferations that detract from the overall balance of the scape,
      water spots, scarred scape, broken petals, malformed anthers and pistils,
      broken or removed anthers, and crooked scapes are faults which detract
      from the overall attractiveness of the exhibit.

SEEDLING CULTIVARS

   In judging seedlings, the primary purpose is not to encourage new cultivars
unless they are superior to named cultivars already in commerce. When a seedling
receives an American Hemerocallis Society award, the public has the right to
expect it to be something to be desired.
   Seedlings are to be exhibited on scapes severed at the crown.
   In evaluating a named cultivar of hemerocallis, a standard has been established
by the hybridizer. In registering the cultivar, he described its particular characteristics. When a named cultivar is shown and displays its "approach" to perfection, it is referred to as being "true to cultivar".
   When a named cultivar does not meet the hybridizer's standard, as registered,
we begin a critical evaluation and deduct points as it deviates from its established
standard.
   When evaluating seedling hemerocallis, a standard has not been established. It
becomes the task of Exhibition Judges to evaluate the specific qualities of each
seedling and recognize these merits at the time of judging. With each entry, judges
should use descriptive words to evaluate merits and faults. General descriptive
terms such as good, poor, excellent, pleasing, typical, and attractive are not suitable
words to describe qualities of seedlings.

Scale of Points for Seedling Hemerocallis

FLOWER 40
   Color 10
   Form 10
   Texture 10
   Substance 10
SCAPE 30
   Harmonious relationship to flower, height and strength 10
   Buds 10
   Branching 10
DISTINCTION—different from and superior to other cultivars 25
CONDITION AND GROOMING 5
                                                              ____
TOTAL POINTS 100

FLOWER . . . . 40 points
In all instances, the seedling flower is expected to be superior in purity of color, individuality of pattern and form, texture, and substance to other varieties in its class. Each of these qualities is to be judged accordingly.
Color—10 points
Color is evaluated by the visual sense of the quality of light which is reflected or transmitted by the flower. Color may be expressed in terms of three factors: hue (name of the color), chroma (purity or saturation) and brightness (value). Color has strong emotional appeal. While color can be enjoyed for its natural beauty without need for reason, the Exhibition Judge must be mindful that the color of a particular seedling is being judged as it is seen on the show table at the time of judging.

Color pattern is the decorative design of the flower. A flower having the same color on both petals and sepals is described as a self. When sepals are a different color from petals, the pattern is classes as a bi-color. An eye is described as a darker color on petals above the throat. Other color patterns are blends, polychromes, banded, haloed, watermarked, tipped, edged, mid-ribbed.

Merits—Clear, smooth blending, brilliant, lustrous, bright, uniform, vibrant, distinctive, soft, mellow; has depth, markings well defined.

Faults—Murky, dingy, streaked, dull, faded, not clear, irregularity of markings.
Form—10 points
Form is the placement of petals and sepals in relation to one another, the definite shape of the flower, considered apart from color. Petals and sepals may be curled, fluted, ruffled or tailored. Weather and condition influence form. A broken segment influences form, but it should be considered only under condition and grooming.

Merits—Uniform, distinctive.

Faults—Irregular spacing of petals and/or sepals; clumsy; malformed.
Texture—10 points
Texture is the surface quality of the tissue structure, the smoothness or the roughness. Texture should enhance the color. Rough textures absorb light by adding richness through the shadows they cast. This is usually true in dark colors. Smooth textures tend to reflect light, which make the colors sparkle and glow. This adds vividness.

Merits—Velvety, waxy, satiny, diamond-dusted.

Faults—Dull, lifeless, coarse, unevenly ribbed, slick, uneven.
Substance—10 points
Substance is the thickness of tissue structure and its holding quality. In judging substance, the firmness and fineness and evenness of petals and sepals are points to consider. The amount of matter and moisture in the petals keeps them firm and crisp. These characteristics enable the flower to withstand weather conditions, retain form and freshness, and give life to the color. Cultural practices, both good and bad, with reference to soil preparation, water, fertilization, and protection from insects and disease, are reflected in substance. Substance with great durability may vary from thin and veil-like, with lacelike daintiness, to thick, crisp, fleshy substance. Good garden practices have much influence on substance.

Merits—Crisp, fresh, firm, turgid, vigorous.

Faults—Thinning of tissue, limp, wilting, browning or melting of petal edges, papery.

SCAPE . . . . 30 points
Harmonious relationship to flower, height and strength—10 points
As a general rule, the height of the scape should not exceed 36 in. However, as a seedling, the scape must be severed at the crown of the plant. The correlation of branching, bud count, and flower size determines its harmonious relationship. Weather directly influences the strength of the scape as cool weather or excessive rain may cause abnormal crooks in the scape which may, or may not, detract from the overall beauty of the exhibit.

Merits—Adequate, harmonious, proportionate to size of flowers, firm, sturdy.

Faults—Too tall, too short, weak, limp, fasciated (two or more scapes fused
together and growing as one), not severed at the base.
Buds—10 points

In judging seedlings, the number of buds must be a factor. Too few buds on a scape shorten the blooming season. Bud placement on the scape influences the beauty of the exhibit. Buds which are placed too close together prevent the flower from opening to its best advantage.

Merits—Adequate, harmonious, proportionate, well spaced.
Faults—Buds scant, crowded.
Branching—10 points

Branching must be judged as seen on the scape on the exhibition table and is therefore a factor in judging seedlings. Branching has a definite influence on the number of flowers per scape as scant branching will produce fewer flowers. More branching allows the possibility of more flowers over a longer period. Crowded branching keeps the flowers from opening properly. Graceful branching is desired.

Merits—Adequate, harmonious, proportionate, well spaced, graceful.
Faults—Scant, crowded, unbalanced.

DISTINCTION . . . . 25 points

Distinction is that quality in a daylily that sets it apart from all others. Sometimes this quality is indefinable. At other times, it can be determined through charm, quality, gracefulness, uniqueness in color, color pattern, form, size, substance, texture, bud count, branching, and the scape itself. Some flowers possess one quality, some possess a few, while other possess the finest of all of these qualities and therefore, merit more points for distinction. The ability to recognize distinction may be instinctive but is refined through many years of growing and judging experience.

Examples of possible distribution of the 25 points for distinction:

Color.	10	Size.	10
Color pattern.	10	Number of buds	10
Substance.	5	Form.	5
Total	25	Total	25
Form.	10	Color.	10
Texture	10	Branching.	10
Substance.	5	Color pattern.	5
Total	25	Total	25

Merits—Which qualities give this flower distinction.
Faults—Which qualities are lacking in distinction.

CONDITION AND GROOMING. . . . . 5 points

Condition is the actual physical state of the specimen at the time of judging. Grooming is preparing the specimen to present a clean appearance for judging. The exhibitor should remove all spent blossoms, seed pods, blasted buds, or blooms which interfere with other blooms. Brown, dry tips on bracts should be trimmed to give a fresh appearance. Condition and grooming include merits and faults incurred in growing, spraying, grooming, transporting to the show, and even accidents incurred in placement.

Merits—Fresh, clean, well groomed, unblemished.
Faults—Insect damage, seed pods left on, presence of insects, dust, dirt, pollen, spent flowers, flower base stubs, blasted buds, proliferations, brown on bracts, and scarred scapes which detract from the overall beauty of the exhibit. Broken segments, anthers, pistils, malformed anthers or pistils are all major faults and, if present, awards may be withheld.

JUDGING SINGLE—OFF SCAPE FLOWERS

Individual flowers severed from the scape may be shown at the discretion of the local flower show committee. The single flower severed from the scape is not eligible for the Special Awards given by the American Hemerocallis Society nor for the Sweepstakes Award. It is not mandatory for single/off scape flowers to be judged and a show committee makes this decision. Age limitation of cultivars in this class is also left to the local show committee, but it is recommended that only newer cultivars be entered in this class. Newer cultivars will add interest to the show.

Scale of points for single—off scape flowers

Size according to cultivar	20
Texture	20
Substance	20
Color	20
Condition	20
Total	100

I feel the A.H.S. has done a good job in preparing this guide and that it is a good yardstick for the evaluation of daylilies. I would caution anyone looking at a new daylily that they always endeavor to bring "fresh eyes" to their viewing and ultimate evaluation. Many times we allow personal prejudices to distort or cloud our vision. The daylily is an extraordinary perennial with great diversity in size, shape, colors, heights—far more than most any other perennial, and this diversity must be preserved and if possible expanded. The judge should not pass personal prejudices or "likes or dislikes" on as facts or learned knowledge! We need to produce greater variety in our cultivars which cannot be achieved without an open and receptive mind; and without a mind schooled or trained in what to look for and what to see.

The daylily is going through a marvelous evolution as breeders perform feats of magic. Knowledgeable evaluations must assist breeders to see beyond the apparent fashions of the day. Fashion seems to dictate much of what we do—but breeding is almost forever and can not be modified as quickly as a skirt can be raised or lowered to meet the whims of some precocious Paris designer or fickle buying public!

7

Awards and Honors Program of the American Hemerocallis Society

The Awards and Honors Program was initiated through the adoption of the amended Constitution and By-laws of the American Hemerocallis Society July 8, 1950, in Cleveland, Ohio. A provision was incorporated in this historic document to provide for the bestowal of appropriate awards and honors and for the establishment of an Awards and Honors Committee to administer the program. The program has changed and been expanded over the years.

The following awards are the official annual Awards and Honors bestowed by the American Hemerocallis Society, as presented in the 1987 second revision of the *Daylily Judges Handbook*. Society-sponsored awards are made annually and the recipients of the various awards determined in four ways: by vote of the Board of Directors; by ballot of American Society members; by special panels of judges of which at least must be American Hemerocallis Society members and the other member(s) specialists in the category; and by Awards and Honors Judges.

The Board of Directors determines the recipients of these awards:

The American Hemerocallis Society may honor two of its members each year for outstanding service and accomplishment by conferring the follow medals:

A. The HELEN FIELD FISCHER GOLD MEDAL is the society's highest honor and is the official recognition for distinguished and meritorious service rendered the society by a member on the national level.

A thorough investigation shall be made in determining the recipient of the Helen Field Fischer Award. A complete list of services the candidates have rendered the society shall be made for all members considered for this honor.

B. The BERTRAND FARR SILVER MEDAL is likewise a distinguished honor for members who have attained outstanding results in the field of hybridizing.

For the Bertrand Farr Award, a complete investigation shall be made of the qualifications and accomplishments of the hybridizers considered. A list of all awards (outside awards as well as A.H.S. awards) and appearances on the Popularity Poll should be made. Special attention should be given to unusual accomplishments such as new color breaks, etc.

C. The REGIONAL SERVICE AWARD. In 1974 the Board of Directors established that the society may award each year a limited number of medals to members of the regions for outstanding service at the region's level. Currently serving board members and Regional Vice Presidents are not eligible for this award. A dual award for spouses will count as one.

D. The REGIONAL NEWSLETTER AWARD was initially donated by Luther J. Cooper in 1975. The engraved plaque encourages excellence in regional reporting and photography. The winner is selected by the Board of Directors at the fall board meeting. Additionally, the board may elect to give a special verbal citation for the most improved newsletter. No physical award shall accompany this form of recognition nor shall it necessarily be given annually.

E. The LENINGTON ALL-AMERICAN AWARD, donated by George E. Lenington, is awarded annually as voted by the Board of Directors. Plants must have been registered and in commerce at least 10 years and must give an outstanding performance in the different regions. The winner is announced along with other Awards and Honors winners after the Fall Board Meeting, and the award, a bronze medal, is presented at the next convention.

Members of the American Hemerocallis Society ballot by mail for the following awards:
F. The POPULARITY POLL. By mail-in ballot, the membership of the American Hemerocallis Society determines annually the top 100 cultivars. These ballots are tabulated and reported on a regional basis. The regional results are consolidated by the Popularity Poll Committee and the top 100 cultivars are listed as the society's annual Popularity Poll.

G. The DAVID HALL REGIONAL AWARD, a bronze medal, is awarded annually on a regional basis to the originator of the most popular cultivar as determined by the vote of the members in the Popularity Poll. The registered and introduced cultivar receiving the largest number of such votes in each of the various established regions is the designated regional winner. In order to win, a minimum of 5 votes is required in the region. In case of a tie within a region, duplicate awards will be given.

American Hemerocallis Society members attending the national convention vote for these awards:
H. The PRESIDENT'S CUP was donated by Mr. Elmer A. Claar to encourage hybridizers and introducers to send their newest cultivars to Convention gardens. This cup is awarded each year at the Annual Convention of the society to the originator of the cultivar considered most outstanding by the attending membership. In order to win, a registered and introduced cultivar must be in an established clump, in bloom, and exhibited in at least one of the convention gardens. (Established clump is defined as no less than 3 fans.) The cultivar receiving the largest number of votes cast by members of the society at the conclusion of garden tours during the annual convention is declared the winner. Votes cannot be cast until the official time set by the local convention committee, which shall handle all details connected with the balloting.

I. The FLORIDA SUNSHINE CUP will be awarded annually at the national convention. This award is for the best small-flowered or miniature daylily displayed in a convention tour garden. It must be an established clump in bloom. (Established clump is defined as no less than 3 fans.) The cultivar receiving the largest number of votes from all attending members at the conclusion of the garden tours is declared the winner.

Special Judges Panels vote for these photography and video awards:
J. The ROBERT WAY SCHLUMPF AWARD was established in 1969 by Mrs. Robert Way Schlumpf to honor the memory of her late husband, an excellent photographer and a Hemerocallis enthusiast. In establishing the awards, Mrs. Schlumpf wished to stimulate interest in good photography and to build up the A.H.S. Slide Library. The two silver trays were first awarded in 1970.
The rules are as follows:

1. Two awards will be given each year at the national convention of the American Hemerocallis Society. They are to be kept by the winners. One will be given to the individual who submits the winning landscape slide. The other will go to the person who enters the winning slide of an individual Hemerocallis bloom.

2. From a technical viewpoint, all slides, in order to be considered, must be in focus and must not give evidence of unnatural or contrived devices such as excessive filtering or physical props (coins, cigarette packages, human hands, etc.). Slides will be 35 mm originals. Slides shall be ineligible if they too closely resemble others that have been submitted previously by the entrant.

3. All entrants must be A.H.S. members.

4. An entrant may enter as many slides as he or she wishes. All slides become the property of the A.H.S. Library.

5. In landscape slides no more than 1 person may be included in the scene. In slides of equal value in the opinion of the judges, those not including persons will be given preference. The slide will feature predominately Hemerocallis.

6. In individual bloom slides, the specimen blossom will be centered. The background will be natural if at all possible. (A slide made of a bloom at a show would be a necessary exception.) Subject Hemerocallis shall have been registered during the past 6 years. Flower color and form must be true.

7. Deadline for submission of entries will be April 1st. All entries will be sent to the slide librarian.

8. A panel of 3 judges will view all slides which fulfill the foregoing requirements. Of these at least 2 must be members of the A.H.S. Any non-member who serves as a judge shall have considerable knowledge of photography. Judges will be selected by the slide librarian and may not be entrants in the competition.

9. No person may win the award whether in one or both categories more than 3 times. For a revised, up-to-date list of rules contact the slide librarian.

K. The A. D. ROQUEMORE MEMORIAL AWARD was established in 1974 by Mrs. A. L. Trott to honor the memory of Mr. A. D. Roquemore. The award is a pewter plate presented for the first time at the national convention in Ohio.

Rules which will govern entries and determine the winning slide are as follows:

1. This award will be given each year at the national convention of the American Hemerocallis Society. It is to be kept by the winner. The award will be presented for the best slide of a cultivar showing the foliage, the scape, and the flower(s) to give a total picture.

2. From a technical viewpoint all slides, in order to be considered, must be in focus and must not give evidence of unnatural or contrived devices such as excessive filtering or physical props. Where an established clump is growing in close proximity to other cultivars in a bed, a background screen will be permitted. However, it should be designed so as to look as natural as possible.

3. Slides will be 35 mm originals. Each slide will carry the name of the daylily and its hybridizer.

4. All entrants must be A.H.S. members.

5. An entrant may enter as many slides as he or she wishes.

All slides become the property of the A.H.S. Slide Library.

6. Subject hemerocallis shall have been registered during the past seven years. Flower color and form must be true. Growth habit of the plant shall be typical for the particular cultivar.

7. Deadline for submission of entries will be April 1st. All entries will be sent to the slide librarian.

8. A panel of 3 judges will view all slides which fulfill the the foregoing requirements. Of these at least 2 must be members of the A.H.S. Any non-member who serves as a judge shall have considerable knowledge of photography. Judges will be selected by the slide librarian and may not be entrants in the competition. For other information, contact slide librarian.

L. The REGION 14 SLIDE SEQUENCE AWARD was established for a period of 10 years by Region 14. The award will be presented each year at the A.H.S. Awards

Banquet, beginning in 1979, to the best entry of slides in a sequence that gives information relating to daylilies. A sequence may be as few as 2 slides or as many as the photographer wishes to use. Additional rules for the Slide Sequence Award will be made by the slide librarian. The entries for this award will be judged by the same judges that judge the Schlumpf and Roquemore competitions. The award will be a silver tray furnished by Region 14.

1. The award will be kept by the winner.

2. All slides must be in focus and be 35 mm originals.

3. All entrants must be A.H.S. members. All slides become the property of the A.H.S. slide library.

4. An entrant may enter as many sequences as he or she wishes.

5. The deadline for submittal of entries will be April 1.

6. A panel of judges will view all slides which fulfill the foregoing requirements. Of these at least 2 members must be members of the A.H.S. Any non-member who serves as a judge shall have considerable knowledge of photography. Judges will be selected by the slide librarian. For additional information, contact the slide librarian.

M. The LAZARUS MEMORIAL AWARD was established in 1986 by Brian and Judy Lazarus in memory of their son, Devin. It is an award of artwork, initially established for a period of 3 years, to be awarded for the best video recording of a presentation relating to daylilies. The award will be donated each year by Brian and Judy Lazarus. By mutual agreement between the A.H.S. and Lazarus family, it may be extended beyond the initial 3 year period. Rules which will govern entries and determine the winning program are:

1. The award will be given each year at the national convention of the American Hemerocallis Society. It will be kept by the winner.

2. The award will be given for the best video recording of a presentation relating to daylilies. There is no running time limitation, but the intent is to produce a program running from 15 minutes to an hour. A narrated sound track is preferred.

3. The subject must be predominately daylily-related. Educational, artistic, and entertainment values will be considered by the judges.

4. The medium may be any popularly used video recording medium, but VHS is preferred.

5. All entrants must be A.H.S. members and must have played a major role in the production of the video.

6. An entrant may enter as many entries as desired. All programs become the property of the A.H.S. slide library.

7. Deadline for submission of entries will be April 1st. All entries will be sent to the slide librarian.

8. A panel of 3 judges will evaluate all entries which meet the above requirements. Of these at least 2 must be members of the A.H.S. Any non-member who serves as a judge shall have a considerable knowledge of photography or cinematography. Judges will be selected by the slide librarian and may not be entrants in the competition.

Awards determined by Awards and Honors Judges:

Recipients for these awards are determined by the vote of accredited Awards and Honors Judges. Ballots for this purpose are furnished by the awards and honors committee at the beginning of each blooming season. These awards are described as follows:

N. The JUNIOR CITATION is awarded for the primary purpose of focusing attention on new and unintroduced cultivars that appear to have outstanding good qualities and distinction. It should be clearly understood that this citation does not necessarily imply that good performance in various climates and soils can be expected. In order to win, a cultivar must not have been introduced before the first day of August in the year in which the award is made and must receive a minimum of 10 votes. Introduction shall mean any offer for sale by means of dated catalogue, publication advertisement, or through printed or reproduced price lists.

A Junior Citation will not be awarded to an unregistered name nor will that name be printed in The Daylily Journal. Judges should make sure when casting their votes that the name has been registered with the American Hemerocallis Society Registrar.

O. The HONORABLE MENTION is the first official "stamp of approval" by the society where good performance goes beyond the local or regional level. Therefore, to win, a cultivar must receive and be credited with a minimum of 12 votes. These votes are to come from not less than 4 different established regions of the society in the United States. In voting for this award, the judges must cast their votes only for cultivars observed in their own respective regions and which have been registered and introduced 2 years. This is on a calendar-year basis.

P. The AWARD OF MERIT is given to signify that a cultivar is not only distinctive and beautiful, but has also proved good performance over a wide geographic area. The award is made each year to 10 cultivars receiving the most votes under the formula set out below. Under this formula, a cultivar must receive votes from at least ½ if the established regions in the United States and not more than ⅓ of the total votes credited to the cultivar shall come from any 1 region. In the event this occurs, those tabulating the vote are instructed to disallow and deduct for the cultivar in question an equal and sufficient number of votes from both the excessive region total and from the national total for said cultivar until the remaining adjusted figures bear the allowable relationship to each other. To be eligible for the Award of Merit, a cultivar also must have received the Honorable Mention award no less than 3 years previously and will remain eligible 3 years.

Q. The STOUT SILVER MEDAL is the highest honor a cultivar can receive and, because of this distinction, the winner must receive the largest number of all votes cast. Should the vote result in a tie, both contenders shall be awarded the Stout Silver Medal. To be eligible for the Stout Silver Medal, a cultivar also must have received the Award of Merit not less than 3 years previously and will remain eligible 3 years.

R. The DONN FISCHER MEMORIAL CUP, donated by Mr. and Mrs. Hubert Fischer is awarded each year to the originator of the most outstaning miniature cultivar as determined by the Awards and Honors Judges. To be eligible, a miniature must have been registered as such and must have been introduced at least 2 years on a calendar year basis. To qualify as "miniature", the flower must be less than 3 in. in diameter. Miniature cultivars may be inclusion on the ballot by any introducer, breeder, member, or judge of the society. Written, separate, nominations giving name of nominated cultivar, breeder's name, year of introduction and diameter of flower are to be submitted to the chairman of the Awards and Honors Committee. The winner shall be the eligible cultivar receiving the greatest number of votes cast by the judges.

S. The ANNIE T. GILES AWARD was donated by Miss Annie T. Giles and is awarded each year for small-flowered daylilies, officially defined as those whose greatest with is 3 in. or more, but not exceeding 4½ in. Registered size of blooms will be the only factor determining if a flower belongs in the small-flower class. To win, a cultivar must have been officially registered and introduced for a minimum of 2 calendar years.

T. The IDA MUNSON AWARD, a bronze medal, was established in 1975 by R. W. Munson, Jr. to honor his mother. This annual award is for double-flowered daylilies. They must be officially registered. They must have bloomed consistently double and have been introduced for a minimum of two year. Flower size will not be a factor.

U. The L. ERNEST PLOUF CONSISTENTLY VERY FRAGRANT HEMEROCALLIS AWARD was donated by Mr. Plouf in 1979. A trust of $10,000 was established for the purpose of stimulating the development of consistently very fragrant daylilies of the dormant cultivar capable of growing in most soils. The winner, determined by ballots of the Awards and Honors Judges, is the cultivar receiving the most votes. In case of a tie, the award is divided equally. The daylily must be consistently very fragrant. Dormancy must be listed in the registration information as it appears in the volume of Hemerocallis Cultivars. It must have been introduced for a minimum of 2 years on a calendar basic and can win only once. The prize is $500 given at the Annual Awards and Honors Banquet.

V. The JAMES E. MARSH AWARD, a silver medal, was established in 1980 by Mrs. James E. Marsh. It will be awarded annually for a period of 10 years. The award is for the best registered and introduced lavender or purple cultivar as selected by balloting of the Awards and Honors Judges. To win, a cultivar must have been officially registered and introduced for a minimum of 2 calendar years. The daylily may be of any size or type. The medal will be awarded to the hybridizer only once. James E. Marsh daylilies are not eligible to receive the award.

W. The DON C. STEVENS AWARD, donated by Region 4, New England Area, is a memorial award established in 1985 for a period of 10 years with the option to renew. It is to be awarded annually for the best registered and introduced, boldly eyed or banded daylily as determined by vote of the Awards and Honors Judges. Final definition of "eyed or banded" for the purpose of determining eligibility shall be left to the discretion of the Awards and Honors Committee. The award may be won multiple times by the same hybridizer but not in consecutive years. Don C. Stevens cultivars are not eligible to receive this award. The winner shall be the candidate receiving the greatest number of votes from at least 3 regions and shall be presented a bronze medal, certificate, and cash prize of $200 at the annual A.H.S. Awards and Honors Banquet. In the event of a tie vote, each winner shall receive a medal, certificate, and $100 each. In a 3 way tie, each will receive a certificate and equal division of the $200 cash prize.

Appendix

Sources of Daylilies

Adamgrove
Route 1   Box 246
California, MO 65018

Ater Daylilies
3803 Greystone Drive
Austin, TX 78731

Barnee's Garden
Route 10   Box 2010
Nacogdoches, TX 75961

John Benz
12195 Sixth Avenue
Cincinnati, OH 45249

Big Tree Daylily Garden
777 General Hutchinson Parkway
Longwood, FL 32750

Blossom Valley Gardens
15011 Oak Creek Road
El Cajon, CA 92021-2328

Barry & Lesley Blyth
Tempo Two
P.O. Box 60A
Pearcedale, Victoria,
Australia

Branch Iris and Hemerocallis Gardens
329 E. Market Street
Piper City, IL 60959

Lee Bristol Nursery
P.O. Box J5
Gaylordsville, CT 06755

Ed Brown
Corner Oakes Garden
6139 Blanding Boulevard
Jacksonville, FL 32244

W. Atlee Burpee Company
300 Park Avenue
Warminster, PA 18974

Busse Gardens
Route 2   Box 238
Cokato, MN 55321

Cordon Bleu Farms
P.O. Box 2033
San Marcos, CA 92069

Crintonic Garden
County Line Road
Gates Mills, OH 44040

Crochet Daylily Garden
P.O. Box 425
Prairieville, LA 70769

Damascus Gardens
4454 Francis Court
Lilburn, GA 30247

Daylily World Garden
P.O. Box 1612
Sanford, FL 32771

Albert C. Faggard
3840 LeBleu Street
Beaumont, TX 77707

Floyd Cove Nursery
Pat & Grace Stamile
11 Shipyard Lane
Setkauket, NY 11733-3038

Four Winds Garden
P.O. Box 141
South Harpswell, ME 04079

Greenwood Nursery
P.O. Box 1610
Goleta, CA 93116

Guidry's Daylily Garden
1005 E. Vermilion Street
Abbeville, LA 70510

Hatfield Gardens
22799 Ringgold Southern Road
Stoutsville, OH 43154

Hem'd Inn
Lucille Warner
534 Aqua Drive
Dallas, TX 752 18

Mrs. Ralph Henry
616 South College
Siloam Springs, AR 72761

Hermitage
John & Dorothy Lambert
Route 2
Raleigh, NC 27610

Hillside Daylily Gardens
14 Linden Hill Drive
Crescent Springs, KY 41017

Howard J. Hite
370 Gallogly Riad
Pontiac, MI 48055

Hughes Gardens
2450 North Main
Mansfield, TX 76063

Houston Daylily Gardens
P.O. Box 7008
The Woodlands, TX 77387

Iron Gate Gardens
Route 3 Box 250
Kings Mountain, NC 28086

Jackson & Perkins Company
1 Rose Lane
Medford, OR 97501

E. R. Joiner Gardens
33 Romney Place, Wymberly
Savannah, GA 31406

Klehm Nursery
Route 5 Box 197
South Barrington, IL 60010

Lady Bug Beautiful Garden
857 Leopard Trail
Winter Springs, FL 32708

Lake Norman Gardens
580 Island Forest Drive
Davidson, NC 28036

Larkdale Farms
4058 Highway 17 South
Green Cove Springs, FL 32043

Lazarus Daylilies and Iris
1786 Generals Highway
Annapolis, MD 21401

Lenington-Long Gardens
7007 Manchester Avenue
Kansas City, MO 64133

Louisiana Nursery
Route 7 Box 43
Opelousas, LA 70570

Meadowlake Gardens
Route 4 Box 709
Walterboro, SC 29488

Mercers Garden
6215 Maude Street
Fayetteville, NC 28306

Dr. James F. Miles
Box 1041
Clemson, SC 29633

Bryant K. Millikan
6610 Sunny Lane
Indianapolis, IN 46220

Moldovan's Gardens
38830 Detroit Road
Avon, OH 44011

Oakes Daylilies
Route 3   Box 3
Corryton, TN 37721

Oxford Gardens
3022 Oxford Drive
Durham, NC 27707

Park Seed
Cokesbury Road
Greenwood, SC 29647

Trudy Petree
4447 Cain Circle
Tucker, GA 30084

Pilley's Gardens
2829 Favill Lane
Grants Pass, OR 97526

Powell's Gardens
Route 3   Box 21
Princeton, NC 27569

Renaissance Garden
93256 G Westbury Woods Drive
Matthews, NC 281105

River City Daylilies
779 Perry Avenue
Cape Girardeau, MO 63701

River Forest Nursery
303 Fir Street
Michigan City, IN 46360

Saxton Gardens
1 First Street
Saratoga Springs, NY 12866

Seawright Gardens
134 Indian Hill
Carlisle, MA 01741

Schoppinger Irisgarten
Burgerweg 8
4437 Schoppingen, West Germany

Solomon Daylilies
105 Country Club Road
Newport News, VA 23606

Spring Creek Daylily Garden
25150 Gosling
Spring, TX 77389

Margaret Sullivan
408 Riverside Drive
Fredericksburg, VA 22401

Soules Garden
5809 Rahake Road
Indianaplois, IN 46217

Thomasville Nurseries, Inc.
P.O. Box 7
Thomasville, GA 31799

Tranquil Lake Nursery
45 River Street
Rehoboth, MA 02769

Van Bourgondien Brothers
P.O. Box A
Babylon, NY 11702

D. Steve Varner
Route 3   Box 5
Monticell, IL 61856

Andre Viette Farm & Nursery
Route 1   Box 16
Fishersville, VA 22939

Webster's Daylilies
203 5th Street NE
Arab, Alabama 35016

White Flower Farm
Litchield, CT 06759

Gilbert H. Wild and Son, Inc.
1112 Joplin Street
Sarcoxie, MO 64862

Windmill Gardens
P.O. Box 351
Luverne, AL 36049

Wimberlyway Gardens
7024 NW 18th Avenue
Gainesville, FL 32605-3237

Woodside Garden
824 Williams Lane
Chadds Ford, PA 19317

Index